Beitz, Lester V.

Overlooked treasures

DATE			

© THE BAKER & TAYLOR CO.

Overlooked Treasures

Also by LES BEITZ:

Treasury of Frontier Relics: A Collector's Guide

Overlooked Treasures

Les Beitz

South Brunswick and New York: A. S. Barnes and Company
London: Thomas Yoseloff Ltd

A. S. Barnes and Co., Inc.
Cranbury, New Jersey 08512

Thomas Yoseloff Ltd
108 New Bond Street
London W1Y OQX, England

Library of Congress Cataloging in Publication Data
Beitz, Lester U.
   Overlooked treasures.
   Bibliography: p.
   1. Antiques—United States.   I. Title.
NK805.B44   745.1'075   74-30715
ISBN 0-498-01672-2

PRINTED IN THE UNITED STATES OF AMERICA

To collectors everywhere
who share with me an appreciation for the
most exciting and fascinating array of col-
lectibles to be found anywhere—
our *own* Americana!

Contents

Preface

The collector of unlimited means—that is to say, one with a wallet that can stand a goodly amount of pressure—certainly has a keen edge on his blade. He or she can saunter around antiques marketplaces, pick up whatever seems appealing or intriguing, pay the going rate, and then head happily back to the hearth with a car trunk full of desirable Americana. This is all fine and dandy for folks who, along with discernment and a genuine appreciation for our wonderful heritage, also have that essential wherewithal, money, and can indulge themselves freely in the joy of expanding a treasured collection.

What about the buff of modest means? In order to develop his or her collection in a somewhat painless manner, a relatively different approach has to be applied—one where wits are brought to bear, where a sort of sixth sense is employed. What it boils down to, actually, is the necessity for developing farsightedness or a sense of the emergence of heretofore neglected items as significant collectibles, and to latch on to them before the big stampede begins. Anticipate the future market scene, 1980 and later, if you will, and do something about it *now*.

It's not such a tough assignment, though. This book, I feel, can serve as a fairly reliable guide to the collector's terrain you'll probably explore. Mind you, I will not attempt to lead you by the hand along dim trails, pointing out each and every little Americana tidbit that's ripe for the plucking. There's challenge involved—plenty of it, be assured. Like the old-time prospector with his burro, you'll be pretty much on your own. That's half of the fun of collecting, isn't it? The other half of this adventurous trek—finding the overlooked treasure—makes the total package a mighty interesting investment. In my view, this is about the closest thing to having your cake and eating it, too.

Acknowledgments

This is the place in a book where the writer makes an attempt to pay off his debts, and believe me, I've got 'em!

Several wonderful collecting cohorts of mine, old friends I've known and corresponded with for years, have contributed immeasurably toward putting this opus together. They've provided me with significant picture material, and in some cases important factual data connected with their personal collections. In brief, they've bent over backwards to assist me in making my way from cover to cover. I cite them here.

First, there is Herschel C. Logan of Santa Ana, California. Hersch collects everything: early firearms, statuary groups of John Rogers, moustache cups and shaving mugs, western art, Civil War memorabilia, rangeland and prairie Americana, rare books, country-kitchen miscellany—you name it and Hersch collects it. (Unless otherwise indicated, all photographs in Chapter 15 are included with his permission.)

Then there is Martin K. Speckter of New York City. I suspect Martin likely knows more about old-time printing presses and allied paraphernalia than any man in the country.

Also, there is Clay Tontz of Covina, California. A few years back, Clay received a letter in a tremulous handwriting from a man who said he was eighty-eight years old, and in all his years had never seen a more unusual trap than the one he was now offering for two dollars plus postage. In due time Clay acquired the trap, and a more intriguing "poachers" trap you'd never imagine! So along with his other collecting activities, Clay is now a trap man with more credentials in this fascinating field than the law should allow. (Unless otherwise indicated, all illustrations in Chapter 13 are included with permission of Clay Tontz.)

11

Nick Eggenhofer of Cody, Wyoming, a tremendously talented illustrator has graciously furnished me reproductions of some of his outstanding work which appeared in vintage pulp western magazines during the 1920s and 1930s.

There are a dozen other great collecting buddies who've come through with a lot of keen-edged knowledge surrounding their particular collecting pursuits and habits and this is the stuff books are made of, actually.

To all these true and trusted friends I say, "Much obliged, podnahs!" If any of you ladies and gents should decide to do a book on your favorite "loot," be assured "I'll shore do my dingbustedest to return the favors!"

Introduction

With a hefty bankroll one can secure just about anything imaginable in the way of antiques, uniques and collectibles. Without that bankroll, there are other ways to skin a cat, other roads to travel, other options to choose. Suppose we examine a few.

Let us take, for example, *Goofus glass*. This is a little byroad in the valley of American pressed glass that is still quite untrodden. Goofus glass, sometimes called *Mexican ware, Hooligan glass*, or *Pickle glass*, was actually the forerunner to the iridiscent *Carnival glass* that has been catapulted into the upper brackets of glass society since the mid-1960s. When you look at this thing from a standpoint of historical significance, goofus has a lot going for it. It is the *original* Carnival glass!

This type glass was, for the most part, of top quality. It was produced by firms such as Northwood, the old LaBelle glass works, Imperial, Crescent, and other fine glass houses that flourished during the early part of the twentieth century.

Goofus can be spotted easily. It is, essentially, one of our many traditional American pressed glasswares, but with gilt and brilliant pigments applied to the undersurfaces to provide colorful effect. To put it simply, it is typical pressed glassware gaudily painted. The decorators used plenty of gold, rich reds, green, and occasionally a sort of fuchsia with orange. The name of the game was to provide a splashy prize piece for carnival patrons to shoot for at the concession stalls. This is Americana with a big "A."

Inexpensive wares marked "Made In Occupied Japan" have exceptionally strong potential, marketwise, in the years ahead. Here's why.

13

A pickle-glass table lamp, circa 1905, was also called goofus glass. Glassware of this distinctive, high-relief molding was later decorated in gaudy colors for giveaway as carnival prizes. Glassware catalog clip, circa 1905.

Upon cessation of hostilities in the Far East in 1945, the Allied Military Government, charged with the responsibility of administering the affairs of the defeated Japanese Empire pending the formation of a new constitutional government there, imposed certain trade restrictions, regulatory controls, obligations, or whatever you choose to call them, on the industrial recovery program necessary to Japan's post war economic survival. One of the measures was a bitter pill—the word *occupied* was inscribed on Japan's export products.

Well, Oriental face is still Oriental face. Japan's national pride had been smartly stung by the stigma attached to that onerous requirement. Connotations of defeat, subjugation, and guilt were all indignities absolutely unbearable to Asian peoples and had to be erased, such is the reasoning of certain trade organizations; and so the word has leaked out that they're doing something about it.

Quietly, methodically, and unobstrusively, emissaries from well-known Japanese firms and export houses are combing world marts seeking the remnants of inventories carrying the oppressive inscription. They're buying up pieces here, there, everywhere for an obvious purpose, namely, destruction. It is their hope, I suppose, that a decade or two of this mop-up operation will rid the world of much of these wares, thereby reducing substantially the reflection of Japan's trampled pride in the aftermath of her disastrous adventures during World War II.

If a collector's bent is toward books, there are some real "sleepers" to be found lurking around secondhand shops, institutional outlets that employ the handicapped, thrift stores, and the like. Two authors in particular have begun to assume tremendous stature in the field of high adventure fiction, namely, Talbot Mundy and Hugh Pendexter.

Literary output by both these master wordsmiths appeared in hardcover editions just before and during the 1920s and 1930s. These hardbacks are being assiduously collected today by knowledgable book buffs who recognize these men for what they really were—outstanding craftsmen of fast-moving, action-packed yarns that will endure as monumental creations in the lore of our literary culture. It goes without saying that anything you might be fortunate enough to snare that carries Mundy or Pendexter on the title page constitutes a gilt-edge investment.

Ladies (and some gents too, I suspect) whose interests lie in early kitchenware, household utensils, pantry accessories, and things along that line, will not want to wait too long in securing some choice graniteware objects that are still obtainable at low cost. As collectibles these things have not as yet become popular; and when a full realization of the true scarcity and uniqueness of many graniteware items is eventually recognized, well—prices will skyrocket.

Perhaps the most important thing to bear in mind while adventuring along this little Americana trail is that of sound condition. Through the years, extremes of temperature and the general use of graniteware and agateware pannery and utensils have caused chipping of the enameled spouts, handles, lids, etc. Once this has occurred to an item, serious deterioration takes place, spelling finis to the piece insofar as its being a prize collectible is concerned. It's the chipped surfaces (and consequent discarding of the item) that accounts for the rarity of the unusual vessels that were created in these distinctive finishes at the turn of the century.

Mottled grays and blues, of course, are the more common colors.

Blue and White Ware

These goods are made of sheet-steel the same as our Agate Nickel-Steel Ware, but are coated on the inside with an absolutely pure ALL-WHITE PORCELAIN, and on the outside with an ENAMEL of bright BLUE and WHITE COLORS, presenting a very handsome effect. We claim this to be the best line of colored enamel ware on the market and know it will stand the test and give the good results that our genuine Agate Nickel-Steel Ware has for years past.

Blue and White Ware Outfits.

18 pieces for $4.69 to $5.76.

Made of sheet-steel, coated on the inside with an absolutely pure all-white porcelain, and on the outside with an enamel of blue and white colors, presenting a very handsome effect. We claim it to be the best line of colored ware on the market. It is as easy to clean as china; it is strong and durable; its finish and cleanliness, together with its labor-saving convenience, makes it the most popular ware on the market.

Packed ready for shipment in three sizes, for size stove No. 8, and No. 9.

To fit stove, size.........	No. 8.	No. 9.
Contents.	Size of Vessels.	Size of Vessels.
1 Tea Kettle..............	No. 8	No. 9
1 Tea Pot.................	2 qt.	3 qt.
1 Coffee Pot..............	3 qt.	4 qt.
1 Sauce Pan..............	3 qt.	4 qt.
1 Berlin Sauce Pan.......	4 qt.	6 qt.
1 Preserving Kettle......	4 qt.	4 qt.
1 Preserving Kettle......	6 qt.	8 qt.
3 Pie Plates.............	9 in.	9 in.
1 Dipper.................	1 qt.	1 qt.
1 Wash Pan...............	11¾ in.	12½ in.
1 Soap Dish..............	6½ in.	6½ in.
1 Pudding Pan............	1½ qt.	2 qt.
1 Pudding Pan............	3 qt.	4 qt.
1 Basting Spoon	12 in.	14 in.
1 Dish Pan...............	14 qt.	17 qt.
1 Ladle..................	3½ in.	3½ in.
Shipping Wt.............	60 lb.	72 lb.
Order by Number	O28792	O28793
Price per set...........	$4.69	$5.76

When a full realization of the true scarcity and uniqueness of graniteware is eventually recognized, prices will skyrocket! Montgomery Ward catalog clip, circa 1904.

Gray Enameled Coffee Boilers.

Gray Enameled Coffee Boiler, with enameled cover, is furnished with bail and cover, as shown in cut.

O 29127—Flat bottom.

No.	Holds, qts.	Wgt. lbs.	Each.
7	6	2	48c.
8	8	3	53c.
9	11	3½	63c.

Mottled Gray Enamel Rice Boilers.

O 29128—Seamless Double Rice or Milk Boilers with tin covers. Tin cover fits lower sections which can be used as ordinary sauce pans.

Size, qt...............	1	2	3	4
Weight, lb.............	1½	2	2¾	4
Each..................	$0.34	$0.44	$0.56	$0.70

Mottled Gray Enameled Double Sauce Pans.

O 29129—These pans are used on gas, gasoline or oil stoves. They are great fuel savers, as more than one article can be cooked over one burner at one time; have tin covers. Each pan holds 2½ qt. Weight, 2 lb. 6. oz. Price per set of 2 pans.............**55c.**

Blue and White Hot Water Kettles.

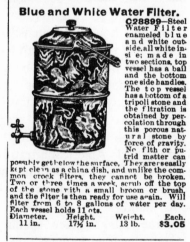

C 28898 — Seamless Hot Water Kettles or Urns, made from 16-gauge sheet steel, enameled white inside, blue and white outside, with faucet. These kettles are being used a great deal in private families instead of tea-kettles.

Size, qts..............	7	9	13
Outside, in...........	9x6	10x7¼	11x7½
Weight, lb......	4¼	6¼	7¼
Each.................	$1.60	$1.73	$1.87

Blue and White Water Filter.

C 28899—Steel Water Filter enameled blue and white outside, all white inside; made in two sections, top vessel has a bail and the bottom one side handle. The top vessel has a bottom of a tripoli stone and the filtration is obtained by percolation through this porous natural stone by force of gravity. No filth or putrid matter can possibly get below the surface. They are as easily kept clean as a china dish, and unlike the common crock filters, they cannot be broken. Two or three times a week, scrub off the top of the stone with a small broom or brush, and the filter is then ready for use again. Will filter from 6 to 8 gallons of water per day. Each vessel holds 11 qts.

Diameter.	Height.	Weight.	Each.
11 in.	17½ in.	13 lb.	$3.05

Clippings from a 1904 Montgomery Ward catalog illustrate the type of graniteware that is fast becoming collector rarities. Exotic tones—pinks, pastel greens and aquas, yellow, and a marvelously rich tan were never produced in quantities as were the blues and grays. Montgomery Ward catalog clip, circa 1904.

Some exotic tones—pinks (a sort of dull rose, really), pastel greens and aquas, a marvellous rich tan—were never produced in quantity as were blues and grays. Locating wares in these hard-to-find colors will consequently pose something of a challenge. It's to be expected, therefore, that in quibbling for the rarer tones, a premium is in order. Agatewares in a vivid, deep yellow will command a special premium. This classic tone is in a class by itself; it shows up very rarely. A single example of it will likely cost as much as a dozen examples of the more usual colors.

There's a motley assortment of air rifles dating from about 1905-1925

Weather Cottage Barometers.

The Weather Cottage, sometimes known as the Swiss barometer, is very sensitive to changes in the atmosphere. It is so adjusted that with the approach of fair weather, the male figure is drawn back into the house and the female figure carried out, but an approaching storm reverses the position of the figures, the male coming outside and the female going in.

It is not advisable to ship above by mail because of liability of breakage. Order shipped with other goods by express or freight.

K11287—Fancy Wood Frame, rustic base; size. 6½x4½. Wt. 10 oz. Each....**50c.**

K11288—Fancy Wood Frame, roof and sides decorated with straw, rustic base and decorated rustic sides. Size, 8x6½. Weight, 10 oz. Each....................**90c.**

K11291—Negro Cabin. Large size, birch bark front and sides, thatched roof, ornamented with ferns and rocks, very handsome and rustic; height 5 inches, width, 7¾ inches, weight. 0 oz. Price each......**$1.00**

K11293—Indian Tepee. Large size, made of birch on fancy base, and ornamented with trees and ferns. Height, 9½ inches, width of base, 6½ inches, weight, 10 oz. Price each......**$1.15**

An exciting, heretofore unrecognized area of Americana interest—Weather Cottage Barometers. You can undoubtedly acquire a vintage Swiss or German example, however they're not always little "cottages." The Negro Cabin and Indian Tepee barometers, never popularly accepted, are very rare. These two thoroughly American *items pose a real challenge, hence prices* start *in the thirty-five dollar to forty-five dollar bracket.* Montgomery Ward catalog clip, circa 1904.

too, which hold promise for collectors. These are mostly early Daisys and Quackenbushes. The mortality rate on those little firearms has been little short of horrific! If they did manage to survive the first time around, they had to stand further hard fare as hand-me-downs to another generation of kids. So all in all, vintage air arms in fairly decent condition have become as scarce as whooping cranes.

There are several other fascinating areas of collector interest which clamor for attention. For example, there is an intriguing variety of windmill counterweights to be found in prairie country. These are silhouette-like, heavy metal castings depicting horse, buffalo, cow, (or like subjects) placed atop rangeland windmills to counterbalance the huge fan blades.

I'm acquainted with a young man who has put together an outstanding collection of old motor-vehicle spark plugs! These are primitive, strange gadgets used to produce sparks for gasoline engines dating from 1905. Another collection I'm aware of is one that represents the several types of cotton scales and weighing devices, along with cotton-gin steam whistles. All of these are particularly appealing to those interested in plantation lore of the deep South.

The collecting of railroad crosstie date nails is building up a head of steam, if you'll pardon the prankish prose. These are little nails with buttonlike heads that are driven into ties by rail crews. These nailheads usually bear year and the monogram or symbol of the railway. The purpose of dating the nail was for replacement alert at the termination of a prescribed life span.

These are just a sampling of things that ought to be recovered pronto and preserved before the feverish scramble that's certain to come with the late 1970s and early 80s. (See, for example, chapter 11 in which all photos are my own).

As remarked at the outset, anyone with a well-filled pouch to back up his collecting whims can acquire vintage material that's already high and mighty on the antiques' totem pole; but a lot of folks (and I'm one of them) have to rely on intuition in order to chart a course around the shoals of limited assets so that they can reach that bay wherein lies the treasure trove. The seamanship required to put safely into port calls for a fairly reliable batch of hunches, a dash of imagination, and luck.

Overlooked Treasures

1

Those Wonderful Old-Time Printing Presses

It's astonishing, really, that more collectors haven't gone in for those quaint little hand-lever printing presses that flourished everywhere a couple of generations ago. I don't mean the fair-sized floor models which had been the mainstay of many early print shops for regular, commercial printing. I mean the little bench models on the order of those pictured in early ad clips reproduced here.

Why enthusiasm is lacking for these distinctive antiques I can't understand. There are buffs galore these days who are deep into the fascinating lore of old melodeons, vintage vehicles (even threshing machines), and all manner of weighty mechanical contrivances. However, there's been scant activity in home-type presses, the truly historic machines that afforded entertainment to countless thousands in bygone years. I suspect there are probably something less than a few hundred of these intriguing machines in operation around the country today in what has generally been termed private press activities.

Yet here is the hand-lever press, essentially a simple machine, which has had an enormous influence upon the whole of America. Could it be that the term printing press conjures up visions of a huge iron contraption weighing half a ton or more? Nothing could be farther from the truth. For the most part, the presses highlighted here are bench

21

Herschel C. Logan, artist, author, collector, and his wife Anne, of Santa Ana, California pull a proof from their Baby Reliance Hand Press. Several fine, limited-edition keepsakes have been produced for friends and relatives on this treasured antique printing press. Photo courtesy Herschel C. Logan, Santa Ana, California.

Home Printing-Press Outfit.

The Outfit consists of 1 Home Printing-Press, 1 Fine Composition Roller, 1 Can of the best Ink, 1 Composing Pallet (2 lines), 1 Full Font of Type, including Quads, Spaces and Periods, 1 pack Floral Cards, and a 12-page Book of Instructions.

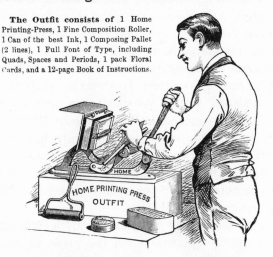

Pictured here is a pamphlet illustration for a Home printing outfit, circa 1885. This hand-lever press with all accessories, including a font of quality type, sold for $1.35 plus 65¢ postage—just about the biggest $2 worth in all of printdom!

models—little rascals that can be carried into the living room for an evening's diversion and then stored in the closet after your printing project (a neat little holiday greeting card or birth announcement, perhaps) has been published in a limited edition of, possibly sixty or eighty copies.

As a matter of fact, the little Daisy card-printer now reposing on the bookshelf near my desk weighs all of three pounds, ten ounces! So let's get down to bedrock and have a look at some of these fascinating contraptions—old-timey hand-lever bench-model printing presses.

The firm of Curtis & Mitchell were early on the scene as distributors and later, makers of some mighty wonderful models. At their small plant in Boston, they manufactured well-made units, employing George P. Gordon's patent design, a real innovation in the field of letterpress printing.

Gordon's idea, perfected in 1858, was that of having the frame that held the type stand up vertically (turned up on edge) and a sheet of

This quaint, thoroughly charming, old wood engraving portrays a home printer operating his hand-lever bench model press. This remarkable little picture is from the collection of Martin K. Speckter, New York business executive, author and collector. After a quarter century of dedication to the craft, Mr. Speckter has acquired the most comprehensive collection of the "tiny monsters" imaginable—over 200 of them! Courtesy M.K. Speckter, N.Y.C.

paper placed upright on a panel just opposite. Then, by pulling a lever, the paper moved over against the type form and an inked impression was "kissed" onto it. It was simple, amazingly efficient, and a great break away from the older method where terrific screw-down pressure was required to make clear print contact.

Gordon's upright principle is termed "platen" printing. It simply means taking two plates, one with type locked in (chase), the other (platen) carrying a sheet of paper, and moving them against one another in a patty-cake fashion. The fidelity of the resulting print impression from that "kiss" arrangement is truly a joy to behold! Some of the most superb examples of the printer's craft have come from little presses constructed along lines employing Gordon's "clam shell" principle. I think this is because all these old presses were constructed far, far better than was really necessary. They were made to do a quality job and simply refused to do otherwise, regardless of age.

Curtis & Mitchell, in business as early as 1847, did not turn out machines for printing, so far as we know. They were jobbers and suppliers, more or less, assembling and marketing industrial wares for other

These old magazine ad clips (circa 1890 to 1920) show various printing outfits. Collectors can learn much concerning background and lore of vintage presses by researching through early magazines, journals, catalogs, and instructional booklets.

*Magazine ad clips (circa 1885 to 1895) depict typical self-inking models.
Pioneer firm of Curtis & Mitchell featured their Columbian No. 1 (shown at
top)—a truly classic bench model. The Charm, a most elusive press to locate
these days, will bring forty dollars or more if in tip-top shape.*

concerns who needed to get newly-patented mechanical apparatus of
various sorts onto the market.

In 1875 (or thereabouts) Curtis & Mitchell undertook to serve as
trade suppliers of the Caxton press, a neat little self-inking platen press
put out by R. Hoe & Company. This fine press went over so well that
C. & M. decided to get into the print-press act with a model of their
own design and construction. Thus, in 1878 they introduced their
Columbian No. 1—a marvellous little press, a masterpiece of precision
engineering which employed Gordon's platen principle. Curtis & Mitchell
continued producing Columbians until 1891.

Another early model, the Pilot, put out in 1885 by the Chandler &
Price firm of Cleveland, Ohio is similarly a prize find today. This press
was not originally a Chandler & Price model. The machine had been
developed by another manufacturer who called it the Standard. Later,
Chandler & Price acquired the man, the plant, and the press along with
patents and patterns of larger presses.

The Pilot is a little heavier than Columbian No. 1 and weighs a trifle
less than two hundred pounds. Cards, labels, envelopes, bill heads, cir-

Here is a model 1885 Chandler & Price Pilot. The size of chase (printed impression dimensions) is 6½" by 10". This press originally sold for thirty-five dollars. Picture courtesy of Chandler & Price Company, Mr. Louis E. Black, Pres.

culars, tickets, programs, menus, anything up to six-by-ten inches can be turned out on this thoroughly efficient little self-inker with exceptional ease of operation.

Flashback: the year is 1872. Ads begin to appear showing an excellent line of presses called Excelsior available from the Kelsey Company at Meriden, Connecticut. The firm wasn't called Kelsey then; it was The Press Company. It became and still is Kelsey—a great pioneer firm still doing business today at the same old stand in Meriden.

Now we get to that part of the narrative where an examination of price data is in order, that is, what the collector ought to expect to pay to secure one of the vintage bench models treated here.

I wouldn't quibble about a two-hundred-dollar price tag on a Columbian No. 1. They're scarcer than clean socks in a bunkhouse. Nor would I balk too much at the same tag on a real early Pilot—an 1885 or 1890 model, to be precise about it. You see, Pilots have been produced by the Chandler & Price people for quite a long time, therefore a later production unit shouldn't cost more than $150; assuredly, $120 would be a hot bargain.

There are precious few of Hoe's great little Caxtons about. Expect to cough up at least $125 for one in fine shape. By "fine shape" (and this applies to all presses manufactured from 1870 to 1900 and mentioned here) is meant a press that is sound throughout and still carries a good bit of its original finish and decoration. Practically all of them were painted a satinlike black lacquer with real gold leaf striping and fancy floral spray decorations on the framing, on the legs, and along the hand lever.

Excelsior and Victor presses, two bench models of the Kelsey line, will cost you less. The reason is that there are more of them around. That firm specialized in this type equipment and became the leaders in the field.

As for the Daisy card printer (approximately 1888 model), I paid twenty-five dollars for it and was tickled to death to nail it at that price because it included all the original accessories! That gem was in its original wooden box, with a neat slide-in-type case containing two fonts of the scrolliest, old Victorian type I'd ever seen. The little ink roller (brayer, they call it) was there, too, plus an assortment of original printed cards and two little boxes of dust—silver and gold—for embellishing the freshly printed impression. As an additional bonus, a neat four-page instruction pamphlet was still tucked in a corner of the box. Rarely, rarely does one find a home printer complete with all these great extras. I would judge the present value of my little Daisy to be forty or fifty dollars.

In addition to these bench models there is another type of press the collector is likely to come across. This is a mounted variety, a considerably larger platen press that has been fastened approximately chest-high onto a pedestal base of sorts. It is a floor model, actually, operated by a foot treadle. Albion, Union, and Golding, Chandler & Price models,

...THESE FONTS OF TYPE...

ARE ALL ADAPTED FOR USE IN THIS PRINTING PRESS.

NOTICE.—When ordering a font of type, please designate *style* you wish by the *number of the font.*

SPECIMENS OF TYPE.

WE PREPAY FULL POSTAGE ON THESE FONTS.

FONT No. 1—60 cts. Figures, 20 cts. extra.

ACME MANUFACTURING CO.

FONT No. 2—60 cts. Figures, 20 cts. extra.

General George Washington

FONT No. 3—80 cts. Figures, 20 cts. extra.

Beautiful Card Type.

FONT No. 4—80 cts. Figures, 20 cts. extra.

The Daisy Printing Press.

FONT No. 5—60 cts. Figures, 20 cts. extra.

SMITH ROBERTS & CO.

FONT No. 6—$1.00. Figures, 25 cts. extra.

Mrs. Louisa P. Romaine.

FONT No. 7—30 cts. Figures, 20 cts. extra.

ADDRESS TYPE. VERY NEAT.

FONT No. 8—50 cts. Figures, 20 cts. extra.

PETER SNOOKS PRINTER.

FONT No. 9—60 cts. Figures, 20 cts. extra.

BASE BALL GAME.

A neat partitioned Type Case, 20 cts., suitable for any of the above fonts.

During the 1890s, Acme Manufacturing Company at 46 Murray St., New York City, produced the Daisy, an inexpensive little card printer of superlative quality. Shown above is a page from the eight-page instruction leaflet which accompanied the outfit.

are typical of this type. If a print bluff should decide to go into this thing in a fairly big way (to produce his own book, for example) one of these larger presses would be the answer. Of course a unit of this type would require more of a regular shop setup; it would hardly be a den or dining room quick-fold-up outfit like the others described here.

About six years ago I paid $160 for an Old Series (1895) eight-by-twelve inch Chandler & Price foot-treadle jobber—$150 for the press and $10 to the hauler. I bought that old "snapper" *right*. This is a $450 machine in today's market.

If you've had a long-simmering hankering to set up a little old-time printery in your den or in a corner of the garage—your *own* private press—well, you'd better schedule a weekend real soon to ferret out a vintage press from an old print shop in an outlying community where the last of the breed may yet be stored.

Your chances of locating one of the typical models cited here are about fifty-fifty today. A year or two from now it'll be sixty-forty, then seventy-thirty. Then again, hasn't this been pretty much the story of all our fine Americana?

The Chandler & Price foot-treadle jobber dates from about 1895. J. Ben Lieberman, in his book Printing As A Hobby *states that this press, a superior printer, is likely to become the top press of the personal printer for years to come. Its chase size is eight-by-twelve inches.* Picture courtesy of Chandler & Price Company, Mr. Louis E. Black, Pres.

I recently heard about a print buff who got a call from an elderly lady asking if he would be so kind (get this, now—*be so kind*) as to help her get rid of "that horrid old print machine that's been cluttering up the basement for years."

They tell me he almost jumped fourteen feet straight in the air when he saw the 1884 Golding in her cellar. As he and his buddy were wrestling with that classic press to get it up the stairs and onto the pickup, the old lady kept stressing how "much obliged" she was.

All the old Golding needed was a new set of ink rollers, a thorough wipe down, and a couple of good squirts with lubricating oil here and there.

That lucky scamp!

2

Aeronautical Americana

During the past few years, an extremely avid group of buffs have been assiduously searching out and acquiring anything and everything they can find in the way of memorabilia connected with early aviation. Aeronautical Americana, it's called.

Eager collectors everywhere are on the lookout for pinback buttons, tokens, badges, plaques, lapel devices, and personal jewelry of like sort, statuary pieces, printed matter, novelty trinkets, accessories and paraphernalia of all manner and description depicting early aviators and aeroplanes. In short, every type of imaginable item associated with the lore of pioneer flight is a desirable collectible today.

Particularly "hot" at the moment is Charles A. Lindbergh material. Emphasis on this specialization is occurring in anticipation of the fiftieth anniversary (1977) of Lindy's historic solo flight from New York to Paris.

A good friend of mine, the editor of a nationally-circulated antiques monthly, tells me that he attended a black-tie dinner reception for the Franklin Institute's first antique show during November, 1972 in which only a few select dealers were "invited" to show, and all dealt in vintage nautical or aeronautical items of one kind or another. A large tapestry-type wall hanging depicting Lindy standing in front of his Spirit of St. Louis was sold that evening for $250. This was an exceptionally high price, admittedly, but the article was undoubtedly a weaving of superlative manufacture (from a French loom, possibly) and not the usual

31

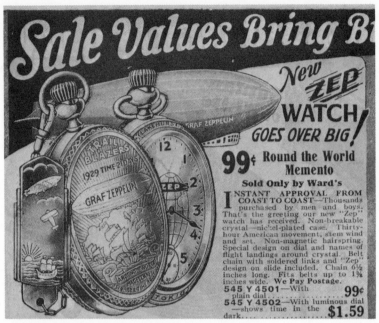

Montgomery Ward's 1930 Special Sale Catalog *offered this Round the World Zep memento pocket watch for ninety-nine cents. The price included belt chain with Zep design on slide. The value now is about fifty dollars.* Catalog clip, Montgomery Ward, circa 1930.

Lapel pins on original display cards always command a premium. Dealers are asking fifteen dollars for this Lindbergh aeroplane memento. Photo from author's collection.

"woven picture" souvenir which retailed for a dollar or two at the time of Lindbergh's triumphal tours following his epochal flight.

The "Welcome Lindy" celluloid pinback button is of top quality and usually found in near mint condition. Prices vary from three to five dollars each. Certain other "Lucky Lindy" pinback buttons were lithographed on tin, which scratched easily and are difficult to find in fine condition. Photo from author's collection.

A big beam of light will be focused on Lindbergh's significant "first" when June, 1977 rolls around. Knowledgable collectors are keenly aware that the value of Lindbergh items are bound to skyrocket, simply by reason of the age-old economic fact that demand will far exceed supply.

The same is true for collectibles associated with other heroes and heroines in the annals of American aviation. Amelia Earhart, Wiley Post, Will Rogers, Commander Richard E. Byrd, "Wrong Way" Corrigan, and even Howard Hughes, are a few. Then there are those intrepid air racers, U. S. Mail flyers and stunt barnstormers of the post-World War I era. Everything in the colorful, exciting story of early flying comes into the picture here. It all goes to make up a tremendous panorama of one of the most fascinating and dramatic eras in our history.

A heavy proportion of this memorabilia, however, concerns civil aviation. Constrastingly, items dealing with military aviation are mighty tough to come by. Because of the very nature of the regular army and its air branch, specialty houses in those days weren't afforded encouragement or sanction to market trinketry depicting Army Air Corps personages and their distinctive accomplishments.

There is practically nothing available, for example, on General Billy Mitchell other than the standard magazine features (most of which are

highly controversial) and a handful of miscellany in the book line—
memoirs and some air-war history, mainly. Recently, however, there
was brought to light an intensely interesting find dealing with pioneer
military aviation— a set of six novels (yes, novels)—boys' fiction thrillers,
actually, authored by General of the Army (then Major) Henry H.
"Hap" Arnold! These six classics in the field of fast-moving air adventure tales are among the most sought after of all memorabilia identified
with the fledgling air arm of our defense forces. Here's how it all came
about.

In 1927, Major Arnold and his family were stationed at Fort Riley,
Kansas. His son William attended the post school there and in the course
of his classroom work ran into more than a fair share of difficulties.
Summer vacation drew near and the young man's teacher suggested to
Mrs. Arnold that William could improve his scholarship considerably by
reading more during the summer months. The teacher recommended
some boys' books, light fiction, as a measure toward improving the
youngster's reading skills.

Young Bill Arnold (presently Colonel William B. Arnold, USAF)
recently recalled those schooldays at Fort Riley nearly fifty years ago.
He remarked that his mother returned home one day with several fiction
titles, one of which he remembers was called *The Adventure Boys in
The Valley of Diamonds*. Since he was very much interested in aviation
at the time, he found no interest in that fantastic story.

His father said, "Well, if you won't read that book, I'll write you one
in which everything that happened is *true*." He proceeded to write *Bill
Bruce and the Pioneer Aviators*.

His father's method, Colonel Arnold stated, was to fill a page with
type, throw it on the floor and proceed with the next page. His mother's
job was to collect these pages, put them in order and do the editing.

The New York firm of A. L. Burt Company agreed to buy the book
when it was submitted for publication, providing the author consented
to prepare others to form a series built around Bill Bruce as the central
character. Major Arnold proceeded along that line and turned out five
additional manuscripts in ten weeks.

The complete set of six books were published in 1928 and was called
The Aviation Series. They are: *Bill Bruce and the Pioneer Aviators;
Bill Bruce, the Flying Cadet; Bill Bruce Becomes an Ace; Bill Bruce on
the Border Patrol; Bill Bruce in the Transcontinental Race; Bill Bruce
on Forest Patrol*.

The son was delighted to have his dad do a series of books with himself, William Bruce Arnold, as the hero—which explains the Bill Bruce
titles. Supporting characters in these books were named for actual Air

BILL BRUCE
THE
FLYING CADET

H. H. ARNOLD

One of the exceptionally scarce Bill Bruce *titles. As with the original display cards or posters which were furnished to booksellers, a dust jacket in reasonably good condition calls for extra dollars when the bargaining gets under way. Seventeen dollars and fifty cents is not too much to pay for this Hap Arnold thriller if it is in superb condition.* Photo from author's collection.

Corps officers of the period, with only the spelling slightly changed in many instances. For example, Tooey Spaatz became "Tooey Spotz." The author took special pride in the fact that every incident involving Bill Bruce in the stories actually happened to some officer in the Army Air Corps.

Major Arnold was certainly well qualified to write about the events highlighted in those stories. He had been taught to fly by the Wright brothers. He knew intimately and flew with the pioneers of American aviation. He was a military aviator during the first World War, and in the postwar era was deeply involved in such early flight achievements as the planning and operation of the Border Patrol, Forest Patrol, and the Transcontinental Air Race.

Having plunged into the book project to help his son with his school work, the Commanding General of the Army Air Corps in World War II is revealed on the pages of these intriguing little volumes in a warm, paternal light. Naming the series' central character after his boy was one of pride and, of course, an extra stimulus as well.

If one is fortunate enough to stumble on a complete set of these six fine items of aeronautical Americana for fifty dollars or thereabouts, he or she can indeed claim membership in an elite society. It's more likely, however, that the individual titles will have to be ferreted out one by one from used book shops, secondhand outlets such as Goodwill, Salvation Army and similar volunteer organizations, at rummage sales, flea markets, and other places of this sort where discarded books are apt to appear.

The *Transcontinental Air Race* title will prove to be the toughest one to locate. *Pioneer Aviators, Ace, Flying Cadet* and *the Patrol* titles seem to have had a good bit more impact, marketwise, selling considerably better than the air race tale.

Be that as it may, any one of the six "Hap" Arnold titles makes for an important addition to a collection of memorabilia connected with the historically important, thrill-packed days of early American flying machines and their flyers.

3

Vintage Air Guns

Among gun buffs, and this includes a good many sporting enthusiasts as well, vintage air arms are getting a lot of attention these days. They're the subject of spirited conversation at auctions, antique fairs, flea markets, junk and secondhand outlets, everyplace where collectors snoop around in quest of distinctive items of Americana.

This is a real switch from the situation a scant few years ago. Then, most fine old American BB guns and other early pneumatic-operated rifles and handguns were pretty much classed as "dinky kid-stuff." Little or no attention was afforded them because there were still some good Sharps, Winchesters, Spencers and similarly esteemed old firearms to be had. Air guns simply were not in the swim.

This is understandable, to a degree, because the Civil War centennial years had focused a strong beam of light on military muskets and repeaters of that era. In consequence, a good bit of desirable material in the vintage-gun line had been bypassed—went begging, so to speak. "Big stuff" had been center stage and held the spotlight. This is not so today.

The emergence of vintage air arms as a "hot" area of collector interest is really not too surprising, either. It was bound to happen, sooner or later, when a realization of the lore and background of these unique little weapons is taken into account.

The idea of compressed air forcing a springed plunger to send a projectile on its way has been around for a mighty long time. As a matter

Quackenbush Improved Nickel Plated Air Rifle,
$4.35

No. 1 Rifle. 21-100-caliber. Full length, 36 inches. Shoots darts and slugs. Each gun is neatly boxed, with six patent darts, six paper targets, 100 slugs, together with a combined claw and wrench. This rifle can be instantly taken apart for the convenience of carrying in trunk or valise.
No. 6P669 Price..............................$4.35
Weight, 4½ pounds. Cannot be sent by mail.

Vintage air rifles such as this Quackenbush model advertised in a 1902 Sears & Roebuck catalog at $4.35 are becoming difficult to locate; they are certain to increase greatly in value in the years ahead.

of fact, air guns had been developed and were in use as early as the sixteenth century!

Let's get back to the current state of affairs and zero in on some of the fascinating antique air guns that are still knocking about and can still be picked up by vigilant browsers who have something of an idea as to what these little rascals really amount to.

Along about the turn of the century, some twenty-odd manufacturing concerns were putting out air guns of sorts. One by one, most of these outfits went out of business for two main reasons. First of all, the making of a sound pneumatic-valve system is extremely complex, calling for exacting tolerances and a lot of manufacturing care. Few firms have ever made the grade, including established makers of cartridge-model firearms. So, faulty design and poor workmanship spelled finis to many early endeavors to break into the field.

Secondly, a lot of shops that got involved in this craft, even though they came up with a commendable product, were financially unstable. They hadn't enough capital to merchandise their wares successfully; one way or another they lost out at the marketplace.

Of these outfits, Apache, along with Plainsman and Kessler, stood their ground for awhile, then folded. By reason of their limited output it can readily be concluded that surviving specimens from these defunct firms are pretty difficult to find. Then too, some of the models they produced were inclined towards intricate mechanisms in the way of operating principles, so over the years the kids buffeted them around and damaged them to such an extent that most of those located now are little more than junkers. To find one in relatively decent shape is a whopping achievement.

The late Walter Benjamin had begun making air rifles around 1882. Because he had both a fine design and sufficient capital assets, he acquired a decent toehold and was able to weather economic gales in the

The importance of early advertising material and supply-house catalog reference cannot be overemphasized. Researchers and advanced collectors who do definitive study on items of Americana rely heavily on published matter of a bygone era to determine makers, positive identification, descriptive data, dates, and similar allied lore surrounding the collectibles concerned. Various ad clips, circa 1915 to 1948.

air-gun market through several decades. Crosman and Sheridan are present-day survivors of the depression years, as well. Early examples of models put out by these firms are, of course, highly collectible. However as has already been mentioned, the real gems (from a collectors standpoint) are the ones that emanated from the workbenches of shops that fell by the wayside. And a few "classics", odd-ball types, that have filtered down through the years from absolute "no name" makers. Take old Gedney's brainstorm, for example.

The gun that Gedney patented in 1861 is a marvel! Look over the sketch reproduced here. If you should stumble on one somewhere along the line, better latch onto it in a hurry because they are practically extinct—rarer than whooping cranes. I seriously doubt if a dozen Gedney's in *any* condition, could be rounded up on a thorough search from Maine to California. In the lore of American air arms, a Gedney is about in the same class as a Colt Paterson in the cap-and-ball department. I'm told that a Gedney in fair shape is likely to be bargained for with an offer *starting* somewhere in the neighborhood of sixty to seventy-five dollars! Anyway, let's stop daydreaming over a rare bird of this sort.

The Daisy Air Rifle got its start through a rather circuitous route. In the 1880s Clarence J. Hamilton, a watch and clock repairman, teamed up with a group of businessmen in Plymouth, Michigan to produce an all-metal farm windmill which he'd designed. As a sort of shirttail enterprise, Hamilton fiddled around with other gadgetry and eventually came up with an all-metal air rifle which he patented in 1888. His firm, the Plymouth Iron Windmill Company, integrated the air gun into their production line and marketed it under the name *Daisy*.

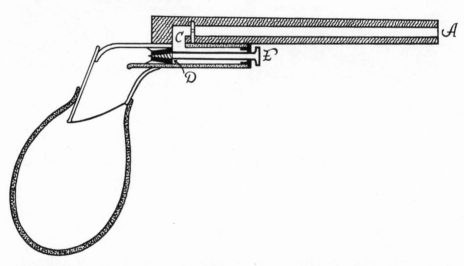

G.W.B. Gedney's air gun operated simply. Using the index finger, the shooter pushed back on the plunger marked E. This blocked the passage at D. A projectile was then dropped into the barrel marked A. A quick squeeze compressed the bulb and the air within caused the plug at D to pop out. Then the air surged through passage C blowing out the projectile. Simple, wasn't it? Sketch by author from old patent drawing.

As frequently happens in the crazy cycle of economic trends and industrial flip-flops, the windmill production declined, but the Daisy had caught on! Before long the company dropped the windmill line and devoted all their resources and attention to the manufacture of air rifles. The name of the concern was changed to the Daisy Manufacturing Company.

Now when we talk about monetary values of air guns we get into something rather weird. For example, take a Colt .45 six-shooter, the famed and legendary Peacemaker of the Old West.

In early 1874 when that wonderful firearm was first made available to the general public, it sold for seventeen dollars. Today, one in tolerably decent condition (original and sound throughout), will bring anywhere from one hundred fifty to two hundred dollars—roughly ten times its original cost.

The Daisy "Take-Down" repeater illustrated here was supplied through Montgomery Ward in 1904 at ninety cents. An economy model of the same gun sold for less than six bits! Any one of these air rifles recovered in good shape today will bring twenty-five dollars or more, or roughly thirty times their original price tags. So when we're inclined to growl about the high cost of living with respect to early Colts, Winchesters, and the like, it goes without saying that early BB guns are in a class by themselves.

Although they're horrifically priced in comparison with their original cost, I honestly believe they're worth every dime being asked for them; and they will be worth much more during the months and years ahead. Why? Simply because they're fewer and farther between than most folks realize and as the true scarcity of some of the earliest types becomes recognized, prices will skyrocket. Remember, these were kids' guns essentially, and sold cheaply. The original recipient kid probably prized his gun highly and took good care of it but after several hand-me-downs within the family and every kid in the neighborhood having his turn with it, well, the "toy" just didn't stand all that wear. It's safe to say that ninety percent of the 1900-1910 guns were consigned to the trash heap a good many years ago; but there are survivors, however.

If you play it right, you shouldn't have too much trouble ferreting out an early Daisy, Benjamin, or Quackenbush model. If you're lucky, you're apt to find a wonderful Webley air pistol, made around 1929, a masterpiece of design and efficiency; and if your hair is parted just right, it's entirely possible you'll hit real pay dirt and bring home the fabulous 1937 Em Gee!

So what it all means is that vintage air arms are very, very much in the swim these days. They're tremendously fascinating objects of an

Air Rifles

Do not expect to get the same results from an Air Rifle that can be obtained from a Cartridge Rifle. They are but a toy, yet dangerous.

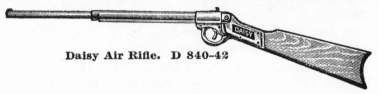

Daisy Air Rifle. D 840-42

Daisy "Take-Down" Repeater.

D 884—Daisy Repeater. Magazine holds 48 Air Rifle shot. Repeating attachment extremely simple. Both the magazine and shooting barrel can be easily removed. Length, 31 in. Weight, 1 lb. 14 oz. Price, each .... **$ .90**
Price per dozen.. **10.00**

20th Century "Take-Down" Daisy.

D 886—Same as Repeater without the magazine. Shooting barrel so arranged that either Air Rifle shot or darts can be used. Can be easily taken apart and packed in small space. Length, 31 in. Weight, 1 lb. 13 oz. Price, each .... **$.70**
Price per dozen **8.00**

1,000 Shot Daisy Repeater.

D 888—1,000 shot Daisy. A magazine gun with Winchester action. Magazine holds 1,000 BB shot and loads automatically. Working parts made of steel and brass and so arranged that any one can take the gun apart and put it together. Stock of black walnut, highly polished. Shoots accurately and with great force. The most gun-like air rifle on the market. Length, 36 in.; weight, 3 lb. Net.............................. **$1.25**

500 Shot Daisy.

D 890—Same as 1000 Shot Daisy except that barrel is four inches shorter and the magazine holds but 500 BB shot. Weight 2 lbs. 10 oz **$1.05**

Because of its classic Winchester design, Model D888 Daisy shown here has special collector appeal and brings up to forty-five dollars on the current market. (Advertising clip from 1904 Montgomery Ward catalog.)

almost forgotten craft and, as such, are of significant historical importance.

If you pass up an opportunity to latch onto a nice example of an early air arm because you feel the price tag is more than moderately outrageous, I can only remark one thing. A few years from now—say

This extremely scarce all-metal air pistol patented in 1871 by Pope Brothers, Boston, Mass., is hand pumped and spring operated, eleven inches overall, nickel plated, with a .22 caliber barrel.

The depression price on this circa 1933 model Daisy repeater was $3.95. It was an exceptionally high-quality product, equipped with a precision sight and genuine American walnut gunstock. Display ad clip, Boys' Life magazine, 1933.

in 1978 or 1980—you'll be lamenting the situation with an old tune I've sung myself a time or two: "The prices they're wanting for these rascals are "Rip-off" with a capital R! Why, I like near flipped when he told me how much he wanted for his old Quackenbush skeleton-stock. I remember when I could have picked up a nice old Quackenbush like that one he has back in 1972 for only thirty bucks!"

4
Lore of the Quirlie

Handbuilding a decent-appearing "quirlie" is no small trick. It calls for rather precise fingertip control, a couple of calculated squeezes, and a sort of lip-flip knack to keep the tobacco from dribbling out the end or otherwise causing the entire smoke to fall apart. With the appearance of "roll yer owns" along in the late 1860s, Westerners caught on to the procedure in a hurry, and another "institution" came into being.

It all started during the last weeks of the Civil War in a tiny factory near a whistle-stop called Durham Station, North Carolina, where a gent named James R. Green had made, since 1860, granulated smoking tobacco from flue-cured Virginia Bright. There was a lull in the hostilities in and around Durham at the time and Northern soldiers had an opportunity to sample Green's tobacco. They liked it. Actually, they were tired of the rope-and-cable twist tobacco that had until then been somewhat standard fare; so they welcomed the change that came in Green's little muslin sacks.

When the war was over, Green was besieged with letters containing money from all over the North and West, requesting his "Durham" tobacco. He really got busy then, and registered a bull trademark to protect his exclusive commodity. Enter center stage—*Bull Durham*—at a nickel a sack, the cheapest luxury in the world.

By this time, cigarettes had attained popular acceptance, if not downright favor; so Green attached a little packet of brown wheatstraw papers

Cowhands used to boast they could fashion a Bull quirlie while atop the back of a half-wild mustang. Early advertising clips, circa 1910.

Sketch from a vintage pulp Western (magazine) dramatizes the lore of the quirlie. Here a lone rider pauses on the trail to hand-build a smoke. Sketch courtesy Nick Eggenhofer.

to his homely muslin sack and offered "makin's" as a complete kit. A sack would yield thirty-three quirlies in the hands of a skilled roller.

In the West, a sack of "makin's" shared with a stranger on a lonely trail became a token of friendship, and to refuse a man the necessaries for fashioning a quirlie amounted to sheer insult. During the 1870s when homesteaders and sodbusters were fanning out all over the frontier, quirlies were actually used as a land measure. Buyer and seller would roll up their cigarettes, light 'em, and start riding. The end of their smoke marked a distance of land in their transaction.

So "makin's"—that is, the tangible items of tobacco lore—can rightfully lay claim to a measure of recognition as significant collectibles associated with frontier development and expansion. There's a surprising array of items that can yet be rounded up to form a representative grouping in this little realm of collector interest.

As is to be expected with most innovations, Bull hadn't been around too long before Johnny-come-lately imitators swarmed onto the scene— all seeking to claim a fair share of benefit from Bull's success. Out popped Sitting Bull Durham, Jersey Bull, Black Bull, Old Bull, Bull's Head, and a dozen others. Duke's Mixture, of course, emerged as something of a favorite with many smokers and went on to become a top seller. (For quite a long time during the depression years of the 1930s when I was in the CCC and hard put for an extra dime or so, I swung over to Golden Grain. Our camp canteen sold it for four cents!)

Anyway, there's probably a dozen or so muslin-sack types to be had, some of which are exceedingly rare and which would require a diligent search to produce a presentable example. There's one rascal, put out by a concern in Reidsville, North Carolina, called Richardson's Original Old North State, that's really very difficult to find. It is so similar to Bull in color and design, that to look at its sack from a little distance one can't really tell which is which; and like Bull, it has the same drawstring muslin sack, complete with an imitation on Bull's label design (burnished gold imprint on black panel) and the same magenta band strapping the little packet of papers to the backside. A quick glance could easily mistake this one for a Bull—and that was the essential purpose of the affair, I suppose. I'd say this one is just about as difficult to find as one of old Green's *original* Durham Station sacks.

Next, of course, there's the papers: ribbed and unribbed, rice papers, straws, brown and white, thick, super-thin, gummed, ungummed—all varieties of weave and texture no end. There are OCB (Old Country Boy) and Rizla + packets, with and without elastic closures, some with stiff cover, some having paper flap closures, those containing one hundred papers, (some more, some less); much diversification is possible in

This picture from a portion of a Bull Durham ad, circa 1911, is slanted to-ward elevating their product into the upper brackets of tobacco society. There's not much evidence that top executives forsook Egyptian Deities and similar classy "tailor mades" to go in for rolling their own. Display ad, Collier's magazine, circa 1911.

this area. I suppose a dedicated specialist could go into this pretty much like stamp collectors go in for watermarks, perforations, millimeter measurements, shades, etc.

There are not many collectors who have really zeroed in on this "roll yer own" facet of tobacco Americana yet, so it certainly provides a ground-floor opportunity for enterprising buffs. A friend of mine re-marked not so long ago, "Once the word gets out on these things, the stampede will be on and then, shore as shootin', some gink will get to printing black and gold labels and riggin' up tags to substitute on late

This is an exceedingly rare tobacco-Americana collector's item. Richardson imitated the original Bull Durham sacks put out by Green at Durham, North Carolina. Photo from author's collection.

Those who demanded the very finest in cigarette papers bought RIZLA+. Ad clip, circa 1910.

Bull Durham sacks. In short, they'll get to 'makin' "makin's" ' for collectors."

Perish the thought. By golly, it seems like one ought not to wait too long in latching onto some of the real McCoys that are still around here and there. If these fascinating little fragments of frontier days and ways go the same route as most other venerables of that bygone era, it's entirely possible some of the more elusive types and styles will be bid up into stiff price brackets, completely out of range for the average Western buff's pocketbook. Is a word to the wise sufficient?

5

Potboilers with a Pioneer Personality

Many relic buffs, sad to say, are inclined to shy away from old stoves. When they come upon an early potboiler, they'll usually give it a fair measure of nostalgic admiration, but pull up short when it comes to shelling out for one. Their reluctance to acquire a vintage stove is understandable, I suppose, when we look closely at some of the monumental monstrosities stove-making people came up with a century or so ago. Insofar as adaptive or decorative attributes are concerned, a whopping percentage of those early cookstoves and heaters are misfits to begin with. They just don't, and probably never will, quite fit into the scheme of things.

There are always exceptions, however, to hard and fast rules. Offhand, I can think of three or four distinctive little "hotboxes" that tie in equally as well with "Los Angeles Provincial" as they did in their original far-from-nowhere environment many decades ago. Let's start with the little ol' *Sibley* stove.

This cone-shaped tent heater was the brainchild of an old-time dragoon officer, Major Henry Hopkins Sibley. He patented his simple, sheet iron wrap-around in 1857. There were two models produced by War Department contractors: an eighteen-pound job designed for use in a two-man officer tent (rare, these) and a standard model weighing thirty

Comparative proportions are evident in the thirty and eighteen-pound Sibley stoves shown here with open-fire doors. Photo courtesy Herschel C. Logan, Santa Ana, California.

pounds for heating the twelve-man trooper tent. Both units stand about thirty inches high, the weight difference being incident to the smaller base diameter of the officers' model. Research of old quartermaster inventories discloses that about sixteen thousand of these remarkable stoves were delivered to the War Department immediately preceding and during the Civil War.

Ask any old soldier about his training days in "tent city" during World War I (and even some trainees of World War II), and he'll tell you those old Sibleys, once they were stoked up good, would drive a "brown-shoe" (foot soldier) out of his tent in short order. It was necessary for

A rare eighteen-pound Sibley stove was intended for use in officer's quarters. The latch device on the fire door was a feature omitted on most of the regular thirty-pound models. Photo courtesy Herschel C. Logan, Santa Ana, California.

Officers at Fort Keogh, Montana, huddle around a Sibley stove during the winter campaign, 1890-91. U.S. Army Signal Corps No. 111-SC-104138 in the National Archives.

recruits to boot a pile of dirt against the draft hole at the bottom rim of the old cone every now and then in order to keep it from getting cherry red and to reduce the risk of having the tent go up in flames.

I know a hunter who has acquired an old Sibley. He totes it along on week-long hunts up North. In transport, he inverts the unit (turns the stovepipe collar downward) and stashes a goodly supply of hardwood chunks and knots into the cone; a gunnysack serves as a cover. At any rate a Sibley is a winner in any sportsman's collection, either in his den or out on the trail. It is a terrific little hunk of Americana, well worth the seventy-five dollars to ninety-five dollars they're bringing these days.

Another gem is a diminutive barrel-shaped stove, a sort of miniature version of the ones used in waiting rooms of small-town railroad depots a couple of generations ago. It's not exactly the "potbelly" of general store fame; it's much smaller, shaped more like a cider cask. It sets atop a simple base frame with very slightly flared legs. Many of these were made in the late 1880s by the Excelsior Manufacturing Company of St. Louis, Missouri, the firm that produced the celebrated Charter Oak stoves. All of these little stoves, however, were designed principally for utilization in telegraph offices, section-gang hangouts, water-tank shanties, and similar shacks at railroad-terminal points and along the right-of-way.

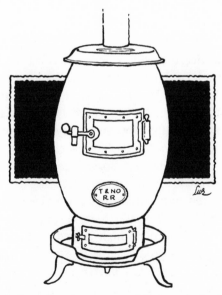

The Excelsior barrel-shaped stove was used in a switch shanty on the Texas and New Orleans line. Sketch by author.

Typical caboose, shop, and depot stoves shown here were made principally for shortline railroads and were seldom offered through hardware and general-merchandise outlets. Wholesale hardware catalog clip, circa 1925.

Anyway, they're nice old stoves and will certainly hold their own in any contemporary interior. I saw one, not too long ago, in a shop outside Little Rock, Arkansas. It was priced at seventy-five dollars—a little too high, I felt. It should sell somewhere in the neighborhood of fifty dollars to sixty dollars though, because they're getting awfully hard to find, due to the shortline railroads having closed up right and left just about everywhere during the past dozen years.

You should have little or no trouble securing a decent old stove to accent den or sheltered patio unless, of course, you hold out for a truly classic one; and that's what you'll have if you're fortunate enough to stumble upon one of those pert, high-legged, rectangular potboilers (a two-holer), that played its greatest role co-starring with Grandma's copper washboiler. They're neat; they have a kind of Shaker simplicity. The firebox on this type is shaped much on the order of a shallow orange crate. More than any other design I can think of, it will do something for a Frank Lloyd Wright interior, too. Be prepared to spend anywhere

LITTLE DOT.

SOFT COAL OR CHARCOAL FURNACE.

No. 6 has two 6-inch Boiler Holes.................each, $2 50
No. 7   "   7   "   "   ....   "   3 00
No. 8   "   8   "   "   ....   "   3 65

Discount............per cent.

To use one hole only, reverse the short center, which has a division plate attached to it.

Here is Little Dot, a diminutive, hard-to-locate laundry stove. Wholesale hardware catalog clip, circa 1897.

from eighty dollars to one hundred dollars for a sound one. They're around, but not nearly so plentiful as might be imagined because an awful lot of Grandmas used the big cast-iron kitchen range for boiling overalls on washday.

There's another washday special—a tub-shaped rascal called Little Dot, put out in the 1880s by a fellow named Filley. I've seen only two over a period of about a dozen years of probing around secondhand outlets and junk sheds, so it ought to be concluded that this little scamp is mighty scarce.

Lastly and just for good measure, I'm including a stove that's *really*

A hayburning stove, pictured here, was used on the plains circa 1877. These are now exceedingly rare; only a few are known to be in important museum displays of frontier Americana. Photo courtesy Maurice Kildare.

unique—a hay-burner. (However, no claim is made on this one that the contraption will contribute to the overall glamour of your family room). The thing operated something like this: spring-backed cylinders carried tubes of packed hay into the firebox of the stove—much on the order of stuffing shells into a double-barreled shotgun—pushing the hay over the firebed until the magazines burned empty. You had to keep a close eye on the operation to be sure a refill was ready when the first load of hay was played out. I doubt if you'll find anything more zany in the way of a heating apparatus anywhere.

6

Armed Services Paperbacks

Armed Services paperbacks are now collectors' items! Paperbacks—those typical soft-cover editions stacked rack-to-rack practically everywhere these days, exemplify a modern-day literary specie. However, as in every area where a distinct facet of Americana has evolved, there were forerunners, trailblazers in the field. Earliest examples of pioneer paperback development are, of course, to be afforded special recognition. Consequently, material of this kind (circa 1930-1940) is being avidly collected and preserved today for exactly what those items represent—vintage specimens of the lore or craft.

This was the colophon adopted by Editions for the Armed Services, Inc., the non profit organization established in 1942 to provide paperbacks for the uniformed forces. U.S. Government Printing Office imprint.

Armed Services Edition (ASE) paperbacks (circa 1943-1947) come in for a healthy measure of esteem among book collectors, not because these editions hit the beaches with the first wave of troops, so to speak, but because they have two other significant aspects—a different format and a horrific mortality rate.

The first aspect is incidental. The second is a sadder commentary, to be sure—but by no means an amen to the issue. One thing's pretty evident, though: ASEs just simply aren't around in the numbers one would call quantity. There's a sound explanation for this, (see explanation below) but first let's backtrail a bit and look into the origin, background, and significance of these unique little literary innovations.

Armed Services Editions were published by an outfit called Editions for the Armed Services, Inc. It was a nonprofit organization established in 1942 by an august body called The Council On Books In Wartime. This Council was made up of American publishers of general (trade) books, librarians, and booksellers. The output of the enterprise (over 120 million volumes were issued) was intended for exclusive distribution to members of the American armed forces—*not* to be resold or otherwise made available to civilians. These paperback books were, in a manner of speaking, government property.

The format adopted for them was decidedly different from the familiar form. Instead of the page size being tall to carry a single column of narrative as in ordinary paperbacks, the ASEs were the other way around. The pages were wide, designed to carry two columns of story; correspondingly, the page depth was quite shallow. Actual page measurements are 5½ inches wide and about 4 inches deep. The book averaged something like a half inch in thickness, running 250 to 300 pages, more or less. A total of 1,324 titles were produced and distributed during the few years these draftees were in uniform. The government paid six cents each for these books. A one-cent royalty was split by the author and the original publisher when work was not in the public domain.

Somebody on the Council who had authority in the selection of titles for these Armed Services Editions was a trifle short on awareness as to what the average young serviceman was inclined toward reading those days. This person managed to put into print some things that bordered on the bizarre insofar as red-blooded American-boy reading interests are concerned. For example, they put out two works by William Makepeace Thackeray—*Vanity Fair* and *Henry Esmond*. I doubt if two dozen out of two million GIs ever got through those.

They published a work called *Mathematics and the Imagination*, by James Newman and Edward Kasner, and *My Heart Leaps Up and Other Poems*, by William Wordsworth. These are undoubtedly fine books, but

I'll venture to say that if you should locate a copy of one of them today, chances are good it'll be in close to pristine condition—certainly not a well-thumbed number.

The same is not so with most other titles. By and large, the range of subject matter was excellent. Somebody on that Council was keenly tuned to the right frequency when these titles were selected: *The Case of the Black-Eyed Blonde*, by Erle Stanley Gardner; *Martin Eden*, by Jack London; *You Know Me, Al*, by Ring Lardner; *Selected Stories*, by Edgar Allan Poe; *Lou Gehrig*, by Frank Graham; *Lost Island*, by James Norman Hall; *Not Quite Dead Enough*, by Rex Stout; *The Valley of Silent Men*, by James Oliver Curwood—and scores of others of similar vein and theme.

Securing any of these wonderful titles in good condition today amounts to an extremely fortunate find, because most of them were literally read to shreds. That literary menu was precisely the type thing for which young uniformed men had an insatiable appetite. Books of fast-moving adventure; action stories; tales of intrigue; plots with suspense, thrills, danger; bold stuff, with a hefty smattering of passion thrown in here and there, were, naturally, most popular.

The not-for-sale restriction kept these books pretty much within the limits of post, camps, stations, aboard vessels and otherwise confined to government installations, stateside and overseas, during the short span (3½ years) that they flourished. Some of them got into USO's and Service Canteens of one sort or another—but not too many. When hostilities were concluded late in 1945, the tolling of the victory bell spelled the end of the trail for this remarkable little series of paperbacks.

Overseas, and here at home, camps and training facilities began closing. At overseas depots it wasn't considered at all feasible to ship the contents of a lot of quonset-hut makeshift libraries back to the states. Paperbacks were therefore disposed of, discarded in one way or another. They were not an accountable item; they were not subject to inventory control—and so *adieu, sayonara, auf wiedersehn* good-by to countless thousands of these fine little paperbacks.

It goes without saying, therefore, that ASEs in any condition are few and far between today; but it is entirely possible, however, that you'll stumble upon a cache of them somewhere or other, sometime—ones that survived the purge—in which case you'll probably want to know something about value.

No title is worth less than two dollars. Some titles—*Riata and Spurs*, by Charles A. Siringo; *Rim of the Desert*, by Ernest Haycox; *The Fighting Four*, by Max Brand; *The Proud Sheriff*, by Eugene Manlove Rhodes; *Peace Marshal*, by Frank Gruber; *The Ox-Bow Incident*, by

Pictured here is an array typical of armed forces paperback editions. Popularity of various titles can usually be determined by the well-thumbed characteristics of surviving examples. Photo from author's collection.

Walter Van Tilburg Clark; *We Pointed Them North*, by E. S. Abbott and Helena Huntington Smith; *Guns of the Frontier*, by William Macleod Raine—to mention just a few—will bring $5.00, $6.00 up to $7.50 each. Their condition, of course, is an important factor and the prices cited here are for good, tight, sound, clean copies. Westerns have been my "cup o' tea" and I've kept a fairly close ear to the ground on these, hence the data above.

A good friend of mine, an knowledgable book collector, tells me that some nonwestern titles are going for as much as $17.50. He specifically mentioned William Faulkner's *A Rose for Emily and Other Stories* and a couple of Sinclair Lewis titles. These are particularly desirable at the moment. Why, I do not know. *Cup of Gold*, by John Steinbeck is an exceptionally "hot" item and carries a fifteen-dollar price tag. I'm told *The Turning Wheels*, by Stuart Cloete is another much-sought item. Another, Ernie Pyle's *Brave Men*, is high on the totem pole—they are both ten-dollar items.

A few years back, I attended an auction at Salina, Kansas, where a big carton, crammed with these paperbacks, came up for bid. The consignment had probably come from the old Smoky Hill Air Base located nearby. Someone bid fifty cents for the lot, as best I can remember. Nobody else bid. Like a dumb ox, I just stood there, mute, and let that scamp walk off with the box full of goodies for less than a buck!

Why I didn't bid on that carton I'll never understand. That had been a once-in-a-blue-moon opportunity for me to latch onto a truly nice collection of ASEs.

And I blew it.

7

Election Campaign Items

As far back as Abe Lincoln's time, a few fanciers of political lore were searching the marketplaces, probing, trying to locate George Washington memorabilia, inaugural items such as a breeches button with the inscription GW. As recently as the last twenty years or so, a relatively small but spirited group of buffs have been deep into collecting political Americana. Diligent seekers of anything and everything connected with U.S. political campaigns—particularly items relating to presidential contests —these collectors have had the field pretty much to themselves. They've gone about recovering every conceivable piece of hardware, software, and paraphernalia associated with early vote-getting endeavors.

At the present time, however, since the Kennedy years have focused strongly on national political affairs, that small nucleus of collectors has swelled into a veritable horde, and the ranks are increasing rapidly. Nowhere else in the world is the political game played the way it is in the U S A. Ballyhoo trinkets, gadgets, novelties, gizmos of every sort (of which the Garfield-Hancock devil doll is a superb example) all make up a fantastic array of collectibles that are superbly unique to this country, that spell out in capital letters: AMERICANA!

If you should decide to launch your own campaign into this exciting arena, you'll immediately have two strong planks on your platform. First, the chance to acquire fresh, rock-bottom-priced material as each contemporary campaign hits the scene. Secondly, the vintage collectibles, from a monetary value standpoint, can only go one way—and that's up.

William McKinley won reelection in 1900 with a strong appeal for "four more years of the full dinner pail." This miniature memento of that campaign brings forty-five dollars today. Author's collection.

This tin lapel tab (orange, white, and black) depicting the Tennessee hopeful's coonskin cap is a two-dollar item. (Photo from author's collection.)

This is the fabulous Garfield "devil doll" fob. A mechanical device, it works by pressing the foot of the serene figure upon a hard surface. Thus activated, the tail and arm assume a most undignified gesture. It is rare and, of course, quite expensive. (Political Americana auction catalog, circa 1971. Uncopyrighted.)

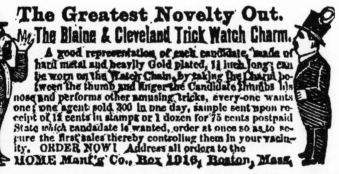

An intensely interesting ad clip from a home and family newspaper (Good Cheer, *September 1884*) *offering trick Devil Doll watch charms during the Blaine-Cleveland campaign. If you peer closely and are able to make out the descriptive details, you'll find that these gold-plated rascals were available at twelve cents each or seventy-five cents per dozen postpaid! Sixty dollars is the least one can expect to pay today for a nice example in working order.* Ad clip, GOOD CHEER, circa 1884.

The record proves it. Consider the following with respect to political items representing just a few fairly recent campaigns.

The Adlai Stevenson shoe symbol originated from a famous news shot of candidate Stevenson relaxing, feet propped up, during his 1956 vote-getting tour. The camera had zeroed in on a whopping hole in the sole of Adlai's shoe. Novelty makers hit upon this in short order and produced some buttons, a tietac, and a coat-lapel stud cleverly depicting that hole-in-sole for its gimmick-worth. The stud then sold for seventy-five cents. Now one brings nine dollars or more.

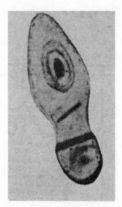

An intriguing memento of the 1956 presidential campaign—the Adlai E. Stevenson "hole-in-sole." Originally hawked by novelty vendors for fifty cents, it brings twelve dollars today. (Photo from author's collection.)

The same is true of certain items that appeared during George Wallace's 1964 campaigns; and a good bit of the material of his 1968 third-party movement is nudging forward in price too. But '64 Wallace-lithographed tin buttons, originally giveaways at rallies, supporter gatherings, fund raising dinners and the like, are currently bringing $2.50 with demand exceeding supply in many areas. This one could easily go to five or six dollars within the next year or two, with advanced collectors hardly batting an eye as they shell out for the prize.

Certain Truman material has all but dried up. For example, one item tough to locate, is an 1¼ inch celluloid jugate button (the term for *both* running mates pictured on a piece) of HST and his veep, Barkley. Current price lists show this item at twenty dollars to twenty-five dollars —and this dates only to 1948!

Some Ike-Nixon celluloid buttons (1952) are already in the four dollar to five dollar bracket. RFK buttons put out during his New York senatorial race, as well as the tragic 1968 presidential hopeful material, have skyrocketed in value. Too, the recent passing of Norman Thomas has evoked a good deal of interest in recovering paraphernalia associated with that gentleman's several campaigns heading the Socialist ticket.

NEVERMORE.

"On this home by horror haunted — tell me truly, I implore! —
Is there — *is* there balm in Gilead? tell me, tell me, I implore!
Quoth the Raven, 'Nevermore!'"

Nevermore *is the caption beneath this 1900 caricature of William Jennings Bryan by the distinguished political cartoonist Keppler. Bryan, a three-time loser in presidential bids, was lampooned more than any other candidate in American political history. Keppler's outstanding full-color lithographed political cartoons which ran as cover art on the great humor monthly* Puck *are avidly sought by Political Americana buffs.* Author's collection.

It goes without saying, of course, that the much older mementos from earliest campaigns are in a class by themselves. William Jennings Bryan knocked around in national politics for quite a spell—he had three shots at the top slot, actually—so there's a fair bit of Bryan campaign material still available at a price.

In one of his races (1896), silver was a key issue and a lot of novelty items were produced bearing the "sixteen-to-one" ratio motif. Democrat Bryan attracted well-heeled backers who came up with the cleverest, most unique little articles of gadgetry promoting his candidacy that had yet been devised—the Bryan "bugs." These were either gold or silver plated (sterling, too) jewelry items—clasps, lapel pins, pendants, and such—which symbolized the presidential campaign issue of gold versus

Examples of "Bryan money" shown here are just two of the almost two hundred varieties circulated by opposition parties during the old spellbinder's electioneering campaigns of 1896, 1900 and 1908. Political Americana auction catalog, circa 1970. Uncopyrighted.

The gold bug is a classic item from the 1896 campaign of McKinley and Hobart. Push the stinger and the wings snap out to display pictures of the candidates. Political Americana auction catalog, circa 1970. Uncopyrighted.

silver. These items are now in the hundred-dollar class, and values are steadily climbing.

Old Ben Harrison, "Republican Extraordinary," managed to place himself in the hands of a couple of ultrasharp managers who were keenly aware of the power of high-pressure promotion—mass media saturation, if you will. They were the original Madison Avenue kids. They put out raz-ma-taz as it had never been put out before—flooded the country with stuff galore—and BH copped the prize.

As a result of old Ben's campaigns with their accompanying tidal wave of hoopla devices, the political-Americana collector gets a real break. Even today a Ben Harrison stickpin (goldish-looking metal job) can still be secured for a five-dollar bill! This is an amazing exception to the rule that all vintage material issued prior to 1900 is priced near oblivion. But I'll venture to say that price won't stand pat very long because the word is getting around; BH items will soon be on a par with those other species of campaign memorabilia we call classic.

Benjamin Harrison stickpin was produced in enormous quantities; one can still be bought today for under eight dollars. Photo from author's collection.

Campaign Goods.

We are headquarters for **OPEN NET WORK BANNERS, FLAGS, Suits, Capes, Caps, Helmets, Shirts, Torches, Pictures, Transparencies** and all *Campaign Equipments.* **CLUBS SUPPLIED, Agts. Wanted.** Complete Sample Suit **$1.00,** Sample Badge 10c., 3 for 25c., 1 doz. 60c. Portraits of all Candidates, size 12 x 16, sample 10c., 4 for 25c., 1 doz. 60c., 100 for $4. Our Prices defy competition! Send for samples and circulars. **CAMPAIGN MANUFACTUR'G CO.,** 10 Barclay St., New York.

Above is an ad (late 1890s) for campaign goods. The line included parade torches. They're exceedingly scarce now, and priced from thirty-five to sixty dollars, depending on condition. (Ad clip, magazine unknown, circa late 1890s.)

Here is a political mechanical-toy bank that is really choice. It depicts a Tammany grafter seated on a thronelike chair with hand outstretched. When a coin is inserted into his palm, instead of depositing it in an appropriate receptacle, he moves his arm around and jabs the coin into his pocket! Sketch by author.

Coolidge had a little something for the ladies who had just won the right to vote. Disenchanted Republican groups put out an anti-Landon pinback button in 1936. Political Americana auction catalog, circa 1971. Uncopyrighted.

Over the decades a long roster of hopefuls—some obscure, some prominent—tossed their hats in the ring with a view of taking up residence in that fine white mansion near Capitol Hill. The political items related to splinter-group candidates—third, fourth, and even seventh party aspirants—are, for the most part, pretty hard to find. Who remembers Wheeler, Seymour, Scott, Breckinridge, Tilden, Cass? Who remembers Mrs. Belva Lockwood who ran against Grover Cleveland on the Equal Rights ticket in 1884?

All these hopefuls had their following of ardent supporters who went about shouting from the rooftops, scattering pamphlets, tokens, ribbons, posters, pennants, mugs, plates, flasks, cigars, sheet music, lanterns—you name it. All these they made, sold, or gave away to extoll the virtues of their chosen political hero.

Where is all this fascinating memorabilia today? Countless tons, virtually mountains of the stuff is gone forever, long ago discarded, junked, burned, rusted away, disintegrated. Gone.

But wait! Wasn't there an old tin badge with big, bold, Gothic letters that spelled BLAINE, and a red, white, and blue ribbon attached? Wasn't it in that old bureau drawer over at Aunt Teenie's house? Better hurry!

8

Rip-Roarin' Pulp Westerns

Pulp Westerns are attracting a lot of attention these days. They are the subject of conversation wherever Western buffs get together and there is active bidding on this material when discovered at book exchanges and auctions. The neglected items of this distinctive form of Americana have come into their own at last!

The demand is big and getting bigger. The supply is smaller than is generally realized. I know, because I have been and continue to prowl around the marketplaces where these pulps are apt to appear, seeking certain titles to fill out volume sets. More often than not, I come away empty-handed because the earlier issues, circa 1920-1930, have all but disappeared.

Why all the interest in these pulp Westerns? Simply because they exemplify one of the most intriguing sidelights in the annals of American magazine publishing. They represent a golden era of sorts, a period in which writers and illustrators served up a savory stew of rip-roarin' frontier adventure to appease the appetites of masses of readers everywhere.

Those old concoctions were, in effect, stepping stones from the earlier melodramatic nickel thrillers to the factual, thoroughly documented accounts of Western days and ways that line the reference shelves of our libraries today. In brief, they opened the door to a broad cultural and educational vista, an understanding of Western history—its social development, the lives of famous men, the pathos, the passion, the romance, and the tragedies of a period. They all contributed to making up

The original oil painting by George Rozen for the August, 1947, issue of The Rio Kid Western *is presently in author's collection. Western magazine-cover art, usually measuring about seventeen inches by twenty-four inches is assiduously sought by advanced buffs for den or frontier bar decor.*

a kaleidoscope that dramatized a most colorful and exciting period in American history—the history of the Old West.

The growing interest in collecting western pulps is just the beginning of the further expanding interest that we shall see in the 1980s. I have been backing my judgment on this point for several years now as I have sensed the emergence of these distinctive creations as a true Americana literary form. It was bound to happen. Here's why.

When an old pulp magazine attains the ripe old age of fifty, it's to be considered a real survivor, a bonafide antique. The reason is simple to explain. The very nature of their substance—the poorest, cheapest, pulp paper obtainable—had a lot to do with the high mortality rate incident to these "rags." The publishers themselves referred to them as "rags" and from a standpoint of physical quality that's about all they were. These things just wouldn't withstand much in the way of use. Pages soon yellowed and became brittle; the gunk that was used to fasten the slick covers to the bulky sets of pages rapidly deteriorated, causing the covers to part company with the rest of the text.

Browsers are murder on pulps. Any old-line magazine dealer will bear me out on this, I'm sure. Scrap-paper drives during World War II motivated many secondhand book and magazine dealers to chuck millions of these pulps because of the merciless handling they'd gotten from browsers. To sum it up, it was more bother for dealers to stock and control these fragile things than they were worth.

It all adds up to a pretty sad state of affairs insofar as the 1920 to

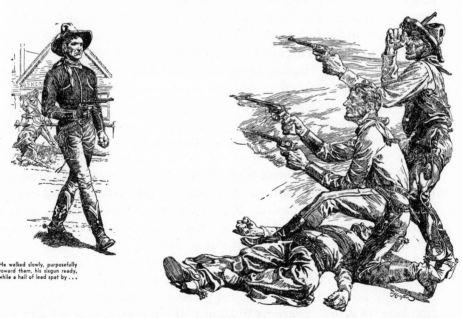

He walked slowly, purposefully
toward them, his sixgun ready,
while a hail of lead spat by . . .

In the early 1950s the few remaining pulp Westerns made a last-ditch effort to retain readership by employing only the most competent writers and illustrators. This excellent double-page pen and ink drawing by Walter Hinton appeared in a 1951 issue of Mammoth Western *to illustrate a gunslinger yarn by E. K. Jarvis entitled* Chicago Man. *Original in author's collection.*

1930 material is concerned. These "classics," nudging the fifty-year mark; these are the ones that are bracketed on collectors' lists as "exceedingly scarce."

All of these old pulps are assiduously collected today. They come in two distinct species: either terrifically good (from a standpoint of narrative treatment and illustration) or stupendously poor. The ones of quality are, of course, extremely valuable for purposes associated with documentation and allied research endeavors related to western subjects. The others are probably considered of some historical significance as choice examples of just how terrible a magazine can get. At any rate, collectors have been latching onto any and every old pulp Western they can find, regardless of literary or artistic merit.

There are those who specialize in anything containing illustrations by the tremendously talented Nick Eggenhofer, Jerry Delano, Frank E. Schoonover, N. C. Wyeth, or any one of a dozen other top-flight men who produced excellent illustrations for pulp Westerns; and there are others who'll pay a premium for anything with stories by Max Brand, James B. Hendrix, Ernest Haycox or Luke Short, to mention just a few master word-wranglers associated with those fabulous publishing enterprises. There's a tremendous story alone in the fantastic career of Max Brand (real name Frederick Faust). Using his own name and nineteen other pseudonyms, he pounded out some thirty million words during his career as a pulp fictioneer—and all of it top grade reading, too!

I've whipped up charts (Tables 1 and 2) that pretty well cover the principal pulp-Western titles and the price ranges applicable to them. It is far from a complete list, but is believed to contain a fair cross section of the most important Western publications from 1920 to 1945. All estimates of value and scarcity are conservative.

The scarcity factors shown in the tables provide something in the way of prevalence on specific items. It will be noted that issues containing stories by Max Brand are in a class by themselves but advanced collectors are beginning to zero in on the puncher tales by B. M. Bower (real name Mrs. Bertha Muzzy Sinclair) and Clarence E. Mulford's celebrated Hopalong Cassidy material as well.

As in all areas of collector interest, condition is most important and a premium is in order for specimens that are close to pristine. There is practically no demand for coverless or beat-up items. Everything covered here, of course, concerns Western pulps; but there is equal interest these days in early pulps devoted to science fiction tales, detective stories (*Nick Carter, The Shadow* and *Black Mask* are currently "hot"), aces and flyers yarns (*Battle Birds, Daredevil Aces, Wings*), and the like.

Tables 1 and 2 reflect my estimations of the monetary values of pulp

An N.C. Wyeth bronc peeler and a B.M. Bower novel are sure-fire winners on a 1916 Popular Magazine *cover.*

Westerns at the time of this writing; and these estimations are based on my own purchases and inquiries concerning such magazines. It ought to be kept in mind, however, that my personal opinion on the matter may differ to some degree with others who maintain a fairly close liaison with the traffic in these periodicals. (Also, the evaluations are subject to change with time, obviously). For the most part, though, I think the

TABLE 1

Values and Scarcity Factor of Pulp Westerns

(Key to scarcity factor: 1 to 3, common — 4 to 6, scarce — 7 to 9, rare)

Title	Values			Scarcity Factor
	Fair condition	Good condition	Excellent condition	
*Ace High, Cowboy Stories, Frontier, Lariat, Ranch Romances, Rangeland Stories, Wild West Weekly	1.00	2.00	3.50	5
Big Book Western, New Western, Thrilling Western, Western Romances, Super Western, Popular Western, Quick Trigger Western	1.00	2.00	3.00	5
Western Fiction	1.00	2.00	3.00	6
*Far West Illustrated	1.50	2.50	3.50	6
*Maverick Magazine	1.50	2.50	3.50	7
*Dime Western	1.00	1.50	3.00	5
*Complete Western Book Magazine	1.50	2.50	3.50	4
*Star Western	1.00	2.50	3.50	4
Spicy Western	3.00	6.00	9.50	9
Texas Rangers	1.50	2.50	3.50	7
*Western Story Magazine	2.00	3.00	4.50	7
Western Story Magazine (without Faust)	1.00	2.50	3.50	5

Note: Magazines marked with an asterisk (*) included occasional stories by this author, and such issues should be valued at about twice the monetary value shown, which is for ordinary issues.

TABLE 2

Values and Scarcity Factor of Pulps Containing Reprinted Faust Stories

(Key to scarcity factors: 1 to 3, common — 4 to 6, scarce — 7 to 9, rare)

Title	Values			Scarcity Factor
	Fair condition	Good condition	Excellent condition	
All Story Western	1.50	2.50	3.50	5
Best Western	1.50	2.50	3.50	5
Crack Shot Western	1.50	2.50	3.50	5
Far West Illustrated	2.00	3.00	4.00	6
Greater Western	1.50	2.50	3.50	5
Max Brand Western Magazine	1.50	3.00	4.00	6
Triple Western	1.50	2.50	3.50	5
Western Winners	1.00	2.00	3.00	5
Zane Grey Western Story Magazine	1.50	2.50	3.50	6

charts provide a pretty accurate picture of the present market, give or take twenty-five cents here and there or a single point leeway as to scarcity factor.

What this all amounts to is simply that pulp Westerns have, so to speak, attained a degree of recognition as a unique and truly representative form of paper Americana—but then, they *had* to. I like the story of Uncle Remus telling the little boy about how the dog chased the rabbit up a tree. When the child protested that the rabbit could not run up a tree, Uncle Remus said, "Well, he just *had* to!"

That's pretty much how it goes with pulp Westerns. They just *had* to be afforded their proper place in the lore of Western Americana.

9

Wood, Brick and Nails

Occasionally a collector of rustic Americana will, after a weekend of diligent probing about remote byways with little to show for his efforts, express disappointment and exclaim that the "pickin's are mighty slim." He'll dejectedly state that the chances of recovering something worthwhile from areas of early settlement are practically nil these days. Well, he's probably right in some respects because truly classic relics of early days and ways are few and far between.

It's likely too, though, that he missed out on a wealth of desirable Americana which had stared him right square in the eye. Some of this material has immediate marketability in its rough state. Other items will become assets according to the uses to which they are put, the manner in which they are restored, and how much cash value the finder puts on "charm."

Perhaps, amid the crumbling debris of a fallen chimney, he had overlooked some wonderful 120-year-old handmade bricks. Or, in the weathered timbers of an early cabin, he had failed to spot some century-old hand-forged nails. Then too, those solid-walnut joists in the shallow loft of a derelict wagon shed may have escaped his notice. Each of those items represents true and valuable Americana and with each passing year more and more of these treasures are lost through neglect, unawareness, or just plain indifference.

A few years ago, one of my weekend relic jaunts took me eight or ten miles off the main highway into an almost uninhabited rural area of central Kansas. The askew, precarious angle of a roofless barn attracted my attention and a hasty examination of the dilapidated interior disclosed stall partitions of ¾-inch thick, 18-inch wide *cypress* boards! Surely that remarkably beautiful lumber had been brought in from a considerable distance—possibly Louisiana—and to have dismantled and rehabilitated those boards with a beeswax and lemon oil dressing would have resulted in a dramatic paneling for den or office that couldn't be bought for short of several hundred dollars.

In a deserted sharecropper's shack I once came upon heart-pine wallboard of such intriguing close-grained character and size (twenty inches to twenty-two inches wide) that I could hardly believe a superb building material of this sort would ever have been utilized in the construction of a two-room shanty. Yet in those days, over a hundred years ago, first-growth pine was so abundant it was of no particular value other than for shelters of sorts. A dozen of those boards milled down to practical thickness today would panel an entire room—and what a gracious and beautiful room it would be.

An early Texas railroad, the Port Isabel and Rio Grande Line, was abandoned several years ago and furniture makers from far and wide swooped down on salvage officials to bid for the piling on which the tracks extended over the Gulf. Small wonder—for this southernmost complete railroad in the United States had been operated over genuine *ebony*!

Another incident comes to mind concerning a fortune in fence rails. Before barbed wire, millions of board-feet of American walnut was utilized in the construction of fence rails. The early settlers weren't very interested in walnut as a cabinet wood; they were essentially concerned with rot-resisting qualities and soon recognized that American walnut was ideal for fence building purposes. Literally millions of dollars (in today's market) of this aristocratic wood was consigned to the construction of wigwag fences.

After fifty or sixty years of use, the fences were suddenly considered valuable for a much more compelling reason. Immediately preceding the Civil War, a convention of gunsmiths met in Atlanta, Georgia, to discuss the subject of gunstocks for military firearms. It was generally agreed that walnut was far superior to other woods for the manufacture of musket stocks because of its strength, shock-resisting qualities, hardness, stiffness, lack of warpage, low specific gravity, and natural beauty. The Atlanta assembly determined that fence rails of walnut were of particular desirability because they were perfectly seasoned from their long exposure to the elements.

Off went the gunmaker's agents on a buying spree to recover those fence rails from rural farmsites. They were shipped to arsenals for fitting to military weapons and were eventually used by both North and South in the subsequent conflict. The lasting qualities of those gunstocks may be attested to today in the displays of antique arms in museums and historical collections from Maine to California.

The country carpenter's craft is still much in evidence as kitchen built-ins such as cupboards, pantries, food-storage bins, closets and the like in many an old farmhouse. Beneath the dirt, grit and grime of decades of neglect, there will emerge cabinet doors, shelving, and storage receptacles of cherry wood, golden oak, and sometimes curly or bird's-eye maple.

In passing, I'd like to mention an "antique" wood of tomorrow—the mesquite. This is a lowly species, a kind of impoverished cousin to the more elegant cabinet woods, but something has happened in recent years which tends to elevate this corral-post wallflower into the upper barckets of wood society. Gunmakers are seeking out the choicest of the species —California screw-bean mesquite—and are employing it as gunstock material for the most expensive of custom rifles. This wood comes from screw-bean mesquite, not the straight-bean-mesquite variety which is so common to most of the southwest.

Now it's entirely possible that this screw-bean species, close-grained and very beautiful, grows in areas other than the California desert, but I'm not aware of any such range extent. Since mesquite grows in such an erratic and gnarled manner, seldom attaining a height or breadth of bole that would render a sizable yield free of knots and holes, the prize lies in securing a piece of sufficient dimension which can be put to some practical use. The real qualification seems to be that it comes from a 150-year-old growth which somehow defied nature and grew with some degree of erectness. The mesquite's belated recognition bears out the fact that the lowliest substance can have a place in the collector's cabinet.

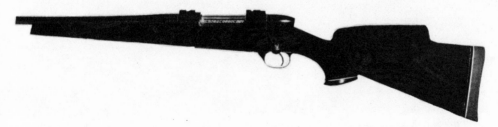

This modern catalog clip from Reinhart Fajen, a prominent gunstock firm, shows fancy screwbean mesquite stock fitted to a high-power rifle. This is one of the most expensive of their many "exotic" gunstock models.

Does it sound extreme to say that an old brick has charm, and thereby has value? There's hardly an area throughout the span of our country that doesn't harbor its share of crumbling foundations, hearths, and chimneys of handmade brick.

No two specimens of brick are exactly alike, either in tone, texture, or shape. Each is distinctive, as are all objects that have been hand-crafted. Close scrutiny will sometimes reveal the little depressions where thumb and forefinger gripped them upon removal from the mold. Different localities yielded clays of differing color and character and it's these features that endow each brick with an individual personality.

Recently I have recovered over 300 fine, old, handmade bricks, and when they're all eventually laid to form the facing of a fireplace front I've planned, there'll be an element of early American life in my studio that could not be duplicated in any other fashion. The tones are mellow and warm—tawny brown; some a golden buff; a few that radiate a subtle, bluish cast; and some of a rich, rust color. They're all just irregular

Cherryvale Brick Yard, Cherryvale, Kansas

This postcard, circa 1912, depicts a six-kiln brickyard near Cherryvale, Kansas. Some of the most bizarre examples of what collectors term "brick-iana" came from kilns in and around Cherryvale where clay and shale of ideal chemical composition produced exceptionally high-grade bricks.

A rare hand-forged nail (beneath spike at top), some old "cut" or "drawn nails," brass keyhole escutcheons, shell cases, and porcelain drawer pulls make up this motley assortment of hardware recovered from a derelict dwelling on the Kansas plains. Although of little intrinsic value in themselves, when suitably mounted on a rustic plaque, these little accessories create a very dramatic effect in displaying homely crafts of a bygone era. (Photo by author.)

and misshapen enough to give them that elusive quality which puts a bit of the "human" in an inanimate object—the mark of the maker.

Early nails are intensely interesting objects. Like old bricks, no two are identical and a varied assortment makes for an intriguing display. There are early types of hand-forged nails that have a daggerlike tapered point. Others, the so-called cut nails and a primitive drawn machine-made nail show up everywhere around weathered outbuildings and framed dwellings. When you do come upon a dilapidated structure that has been built from foundation to rooftop with various sizes of spikes, nails, and brads, you can gather an almost complete collection of nail varieties. In pursuing a cache of old nails, it's either feast or famine.

Wherever old nails and spikes appear, there's bound to be other fastenings and hardware that clamor for attention. Broken cabinet doors will often yield early hinge devices, latches and catches of sorts, and the drawers of rickety chests frequently have decorative bales and keyhole escutcheons of hand-wrought construction.

The fascinating little porcelain drawer pulls seem to show up everywhere around abandoned farmhouses, particularly in and about long-vacated general-store sites. These knobs were used extensively on bin drawers, spice and spool cabinets, tea cannisters and various other compartment-type storage pieces that were part and parcel of community trade centers a couple of generations ago. I have a jim-dandy of a bunkhouse door latch which was recovered from the shambles of such a structure miles from nowhere on the Kansas prairie. There's just no end to the intriguing little accessories and fittings one will find tenaciously clinging to old cabinetwood, shelving, door frames, and on decaying rafters and sills.

The long-forsaken structures which still silhouette the horizons of our desolate landscapes shelter the antiques of tomorrow. They may appear at first glance to be quite commonplace, even homely, and of such crude and rustic character as to be termed undistinguished; but who would ever have figured that a buffalo skull, an old muleshoe or a strand of early-frontier experimental barbed wire would today constitute an important historical link with the western panorama of a century ago?

Next time you turn off a main highway and wind through the backroads of rural communities in quest of things quaint, be aware of any old, abandoned structure you see. You'll find brick and nails and finely-figured old wood, I'm sure. I have—and my eyesight isn't what you'd call a gilt-edge asset for such purposes, either!

10

Arbuckle Coffee Memorabilia

Hosteen Cohay! That's what long-haired Navajos uttered when they bargained with Indian traders for Arbuckle coffee. Translated, it means "Mr. Coffee"—and that means John Arbuckle.

John had gotten into the coffee business in a big way shortly after the close of the Civil War. By reason of his remarkable ingenuity in perfecting a glazing process to seal in the flavor of freshly roasted coffee beans (along with some mighty sharp merchandising practices), he and his brother Charles succeeded in making the flying-angel trademark the symbol for good coffee everywhere.

With a keen eye on the rapidly expanding trade areas opening up throughout the far West, they saw to it that every wagon freighter and train of boxcars heading in that direction had plenty of *Ariosa* (Arbuckle coffee trade name). In brief, the Arbuckle boys had come up with a product much in demand and they proceeded to deliver it wherever the demand existed. Actually, they had three things going for them.

First, their coffee was good. Secondly, in prairie country where wood was scarce, Arbuckle shipping boxes were important items of salvage. Homesteaders knocked out the ends and used them for well casings. Post traders used them for shelving, bins, chests, and storage containers of all sorts. Indian women used them for cradle boards, decorated with buckskin and silver. They also wound up being used for packsaddle panniers, feed boxes, furniture, doors, and coffins, too. You name it, and

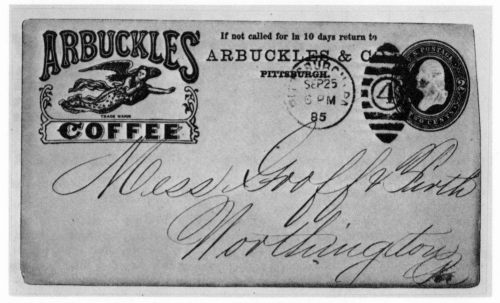

A business envelope highlights the "flying angel" trademark, the symbol for good coffee throughout the expanding frontier. Picture courtesy Kit Vickrey; Joplin, Missouri.

This wooden packing case is a scarce item of Arbuckliana. Round-up chuck-wagon boxes made from these old cases are much sought after by collectors of frontier Americana. Photo courtesy Major and Virginia Bruton.

an Arbuckle packing case would make it. One of the nicest old chuck-wagon grub boxes I ever saw was made by an old-time ranch handyman from a couple of those sturdy cases.

Lastly, there were the coupons—or, more appropriately, the things you got for the coupons. There's just no way of estimating how many thousands of pairs of wide suspenders worn by hard-slogging ranchmen and sodbusters were ordered from Arbuckle premium catalogues. Old company records show, among other intensely interesting things, that a couple of hundred-thousand fine quality straight razors were sent out in redemption of Ariosa coupons; and, as might be supposed, coffee grinders went out by the thousands. Hefty pocket knives, watches, pots, pans, dolls, polka-dot handkerchiefs, rings, scissors—just about everything a Westerner wanted or needed (except firearms) were included on Arbuckle premium leaflets.

All in all, the Arbuckle enterprise in the marketing of coffee resulted in what you might call an "institution" in the West; and their homely little coupons, Ariosa packages, fancy stencilled (japanned) store-front

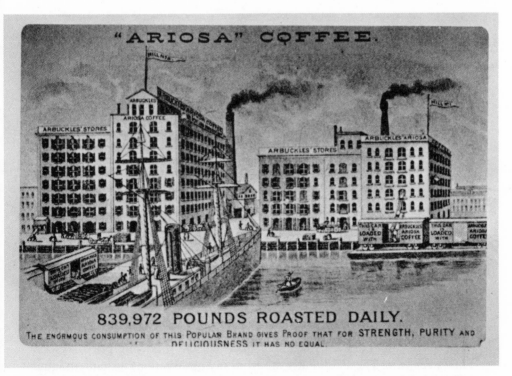

The advertising "trade" card above depicts bustling activity around Arbuckle roasting mills in Pittsburgh during the 1880s.

A label on a one-pound bag of famed Arbuckle ground coffee and a coupon snipped from package are pictured here. Label courtesy Kit Vickrey and Ariosa coupon from author's collection.

signs, counter-display placards, shipping cases, premium lists, and the like make up a unique area of collector interest.

The store signs show up from time to time when old stockrooms or warehouses are renovated. Shipping cases can sometimes be located, but they're usually in a knocked down state, still doing good service as interior partitioning in stables and sheds. Occasionally when the far reaches of an old closet or trunk have been penetrated, a packet of Ariosa coupons comes to light. Even a few unopened one-pound bags of the aromatic brew, which years ago had been sealed and stashed in pantry corners have lately been recovered.

A fair share of all these wonderful Arbuckle items are still around, but I won't go so far as to say they're plentiful. Elusive is a better way to put it. Anyway, keep an eye peeled because sooner or later you'll run up on a genuine bit of "Arbuckliana"—and that spells *bonus points* in any collection of things American.

Although the somewhat offbeat, even nondescript nature of many of these pioneer coffee collectibles has created a rather fuzzy situation with respect to prices dealers ask for them, I feel the following price tags are fairly realistic. These estimates are from my observations around antiques marketplaces where an occasional "Arbuckliana" item has appeared.

Ariosa premium coupons go for about one dollar apiece. A one-pound paper carton for genuine, honest-to-goodness old Ariosa will bring from $3.50 to $4.50; a hundred-carton wooden packing case, twenty dollars—perhaps twenty-five dollars—certainly no more. I recently saw one priced at thirty-five dollars, which was too high for it, I felt. The fact that the dealer still has it, unable to move it along at that price, tends to bear out my opinion.

A six-page list of Arbuckle premiums, in nice condition, should be worth four or five dollars. Small merchant's display signs, counter size, are well worth the fifteen to twenty dollars being asked for them.

In case you've wondered what the Arbuckle trade-name Ariosa stands for, here is an explanation I read somewhere a long time ago, which may or may not be historically accurate. It is simply offered as a possibility.

A, is for Arbuckle; RIO, for the region it came from in SA, South America. Makes sense, I suppose—or does it?

11

Stirrups, Bits and Spurs

The "Hosses" Went West

Anyone who knows beans from buckshot about the old West will tell you there's a right smart difference between a "hoss" and a horse. A horse eats cultivated grains and sun-cured hay, is occasionally treated to a juicy apple or a lump of sugar. He is sleek, the result of meticulous currying, with special attention devoted to the grooming of mane and tail. Should he get a slight chill, he is blanketed and put in a warm barn. A veterinarian is summoned.

Now a "hoss" eats wild grasses and the coarse foliage that grows on scrublands and along rocky ledges of desolate canyons. Now and then he'll nibble more than a fair share of locoweed, too. He is picketed out at night and though it storm and sleet something fierce, comes morning he'll amble in with the rest of the *remuda*, ("herd") looking little the worse for the harsh elements. Then he'll go about his business and turn in a good day's work for his rider.

Horses didn't go West—"hosses" did!

Hosses (mules and oxen, too) have far more to do with the lore of the old frontier than many would imagine. Western historians have gone overboard in their emphasis on Western personality and character types, and there's been comprehensive coverage of rip-roaring towns and camps; but the archives are pretty lean in acknowledgment of or tribute to the animals that bore, guided, and hauled those adventurous people and their cargoes westward more than a century ago. Skimpier still is men-

92

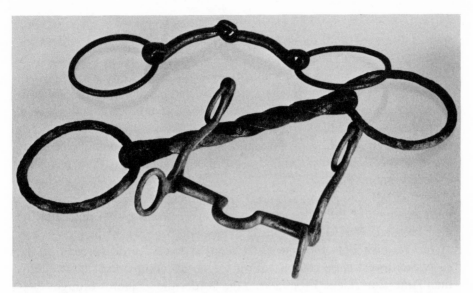

*These old bits—the snaffle or linked bit (upper), bar bit, and Texas model—
were all prevalent throughout the West.*

*These are cavalry spurs of the Custer era. The brass one in the foreground is
an officer's issue. An enlisted trooper wore the iron spur which still has a
portion of the original strap attached.*

tion of the gear and accessories associated with those bold endeavors, things that are truly as significant to the panorama of the untamed frontier as were the colorful personalities and places.

The Conestoga wagons, longhorn steers, and cavalry outposts are gone now, but there's still a fair showing of old stirrups, bits, and spurs in and around abandoned wagon sheds, line shacks, and derelict corrals from Missouri to California. They're fascinating fragments of early Western days and ways, and deserve more recognition than has been afforded them.

First of all, something should be said about the *vaquero* ("cowboy") because much of the lore of the open range centers around him and the gear he used. Here again, historians have been negligent in recognition of the Spanish horsemen; actually a great many cattle spreads of the early Southwest were staffed with a far larger complement of vaqueros than American riders. From across the border the vaqueros brought their traditional equipment, and here's where we find some of the most ornate and stylized trappings in the entire realm of horse gear.

The Chihuahua spur is a proper example. It has heft, embodying much of that bold but graceful solidity we see in the heavily molded character-

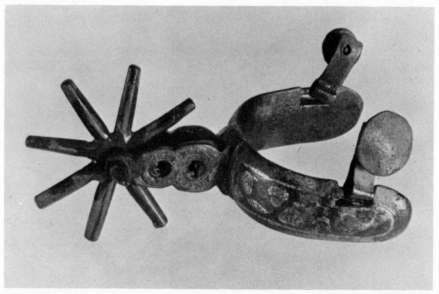

The Chihuahua spur is closely identified with the vaqueros *(cowboys) and riders of Southwestern border country. This example is plain as compared to other very ornately crafted examples. The huge rowel and the gold and silver inlay are characteristics of Spanish-type spurs.*

These boxcars, (usually called box stirrups) tell a story of long, hard days on the trail. Note the worn tread on the one in the foreground.

istics of traditional Spanish furniture. Although massive in concept, these spurs exemplify a highly decorative quality in their silver inlay and the grand spangle of the spur wheels (rowels, they're called), which are as much as three inches in diameter. Nothing about this spur could be called conservative, and for good reason. They are intended to enforce some degree of compliance from half-wild mustangs and they certainly did the job. The same is true of ring-and-spade bits. They too are of strong Spanish influence, and designed to control mounts not always compatible with their riders' intention.

The boxcar, or box stirrup, might well serve to round out this brief description of vaquero horse gear. Although cumbersome in appearance, these stirrups were expressly suited to the vaquero's riding style—his technique in the saddle, so to speak. They're an adaptation of the older Spanish one-piece wooden stirrup (called the doghouse) and the tread on some of these monstrosities is quite wide—six inches or so.

The vaqueros of the border country were tradition bound and they clung to some old-world principles in the handling of range ponies that were at great variance with those employed by the American cowboy. Boxcars were favored by the vaqueros long after our waddies (cowboys) had adopted stirrups of more practical size, shape, and weight. So these distinctive items—the Chihuahua, spade and ring bits, and the boxcar stirrup were first on the scene in the days when riders and longhorn critters were the dominant factors of the great cattle empires.

Now the waddy, the American cowboy, performed quite well with a somewhat more modified set of gear. His spurs, for example, were likely to be the famous OK variety—a sensible, practical spur that was far less severe as a goading device than the earlier Spanish types. Many of the old-time cowboys first broke out with a pair of OK's and, to this day, adaptations of that favorite type are prevalent throughout Western rangelands. OK's were appropriate to the business at hand because the waddy's mount was, for the most part, fairly well disciplined and responded to gentler treatment.

The famous OK spur was exceptionally popular with working cowhands. Its practical design was adaptable to the general conditions of everyday range life.

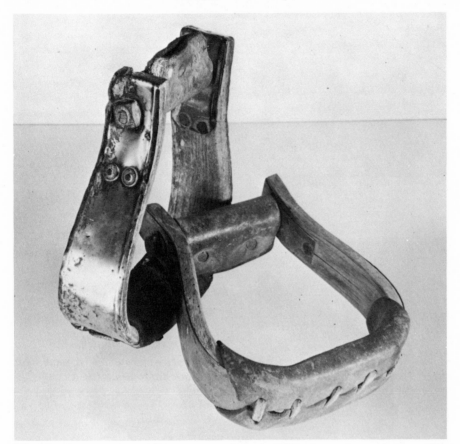

The Visalia was one of the most popular of all Western-stirrup designs. The upright one has a light-gage brass facing; the other is faced with galvanized tin.

As to stirrups, the Visalia was a happy medium between the clumsy box stirrup and the trim military models. It came to be accepted in cattle country as an all-around favorite and has remained so today. It is, of course, lighter than the boxy, doghouse types favored by the vaqueros and provides for a fuller grip on the tread when "cutting out" and working close to the herd. The oxbow provided even more grip and was particulary useful to rough-string riders—bronc peelers—who needed every speck of grip they could get.

This is, of course, a very limited rundown on just a few typical items associated with range life and is intended merely to serve as an introduction to a most fascinating area of collector interest. As to monetary

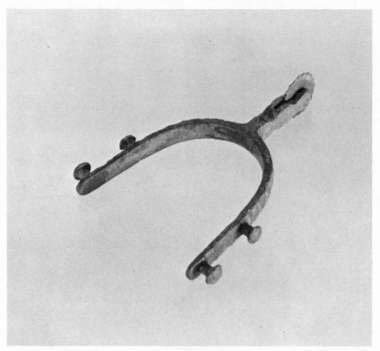

This old straight-shank spur with sawtooth rowel was found in a trash heap near Austin, Texas. It appears to be much more appropriate for a gentleman rider than for cowboys with half-wild mustangs.

value—and something should be mentioned along this line since folks do buy and sell these relics—there is hardly a single item in the lot that currently brings more than ten dollars. This is a tremendous opportunity for the collector! I have a 100-year-old-plus vaquero spur with silver and gold inlay that cost me six dollars a year ago—and the dealer made a profit!

My particular affection for these lowly objects, insignificant as they may appear to be, stems from a sincere recognition of the role they played in the Old West. I have no quarrel with Colonel Joe Miller's ten-thousand dollar silver-mounted saddle nor the fabulous worth of Buffalo Bill's expertly engraved Winchester '73. I simply think the old bit I'm looking at right now is a mite closer to the pulse of that colorful and exciting period in our history. I like horses; but I have a downright special admiration for a "hoss!"

12

Country Cabinets

Every early kitchen had a couple of cabinets for the storage of tableware, utensils, certain foodstuffs and the like. With all the bugs and varmints snooping in and around those places in those days, secure storage was absolutely essential. Open shelving along a side wall or in a corner had some measure of practical purpose in earlier pioneer households, but by and large a closed cabinet became the real answer to storage problems, particularly for those involving food.

Typical was the food safe, sometimes called a milk safe, pie safe, jelly cupboard, or just plain kitchen cabinet. There are two types you're likely to find. The more common is a rather tall unit, six feet or thereabouts; the other, a shorter specie—a squat, boxy affair mounted atop slender legs that are about eighteen or twenty inches off the floor.

The taller ones have been well described in articles and features dealing with country furniture; so there's little need to go into a lengthy discussion about them here. Let's keep in mind however, that they're especially nice for general utility, storage, or display cabinets. Valuewise, if you're bargaining for one that's in reasonably decent shape, the tab ought to be in the neighborhood of sixty to seventy-five dollars. For this price the overall framing should be sound and the decorative pierced-tin side panels, (frequently used on the doors, too), should be in reasonably rust-free condition. One always expects to have to refinish these cabinets, and to replace a door knob, a hinge or two, perhaps, and possibly the

Most food safes (often called pie safes) had perforated-tin ventilator panels on the sides and sometimes on the doors. This one, of golden oak, has thin, wooden, side ventilators with typical Victorian designs depressed into the upper-door panels.

drawer pulls. Pine, poplar, and what is being called "golden oak," were used quite extensively in the crafting of these cabinets; but occasionally one of walnut or cherrywood will show up. These finer-quality cabinet-wood specimens are likely to run in the one-hundred-fifty to two-hundred-dollar bracket when the haggling gets serious.

Most of these taller cupboards and cabinets cited here were made in towns located near heavily timbered regions along the Atlantic seaboard —the Carolinas, Maryland, West Virginia, and Virginia. Some came from Tennessee, too. They had been shipped to Memphis, St. Louis, and Kansas City for marketing from these points. Also because these cabinets were more usual, or more popular, they are not so scarce that they cannot still be found in and about rural communities throughout the Midwest and Southwest. The same is not true for the shorter ones mentioned above, however. These are a different story, and here it is.

Furniture houses at terminal points near the fringe of the newly-opened homestead lands (in and around Omaha, Topeka, even Little Rock, Arkansas and places like that), began to get orders for kitchen cabinets, so-called dry sinks, water benches (a type of basin stand usually found on back porches or in wash-up sheds, built rather low to permit bending over while scrubbing and rinsing face and hands), washstands, and similar furnishings. These were intended for shipment further west-ward where the demand was increasing. About the only cabinetmakers around those towns at the time were some German and Scandinavian immigrants looking for opportunity. They were promptly put to work in local woodshops, turning out these utilitarian items for the rapidly expanding market. However, these craftsmen had ideas of their own as to how a household cabinet ought to be framed and mounted: on legs—like lowboys, consoles, or any of the other chest and bureaulike storage units they'd made and used for generations back in the old country. That's how these unique high-legged food safes found their way onto the frontier; they were supplemental product to the more usual Eastern types.

In one way or another, a high percentage of these Dutch-looking food safes followed trails into Texas. I've seen a few in Kansas and a couple in Oklahoma shops during the past year or so; and I spotted one in an Arkansas antique outlet recently. The German and Norwegian settle-ments in Texas, however, showed a decided preference for them and that's usually where they are found. One thing is certain—they were never produced in quantity. Consequently, one in good shape is quite a find; and because of this scarcity factor, it will bring every bit as much as professionally crafted cabinets of walnut, figured maple, poplar, or cherry.

Although pert, high-legged kitchen cabinets such as this one are sometimes referred to as jelly cupboards, the pierced ventilator panels suggest they were intended chiefly for storage of fresh garden produce, eggs, cheeses, and the like. An old furniture-supply-house catalog dated 1891 illustrates a similar type which they referred to as a bread or pastry chest. Furniture-catalog clip, circa 1900.

Next we come to corner cupboards—corner closets, some folks call them. Hardly any of these three-sided cabinets were crafted in or around frontier settlements. When they show up near early homestead communities, it's because they were brought in by settlers from Pennsylvania and the Ohio Valley on emigrant treks westward.

Usually, they're cabinet-on-cabinet affairs—that is, two-piece units. The upper portion, when placed angle-back to the lower section, shaped up as a box. This facilitated storage in a wagon. The packing of personal things was a reality factor aboard prairie schooners; so it isn't surprising that settlers considered these corner cabinets to be of great utilitarian value on the trip, as well as a worthwhile furnishing in their new homes.

Those I've seen were mostly of cherrywood or heart pine. They're scarce; and, because most of them had served for a generation or two prior to heading west they have the element of antiquity. Therefore, they are also high priced.

It goes without saying, early corner cupboards are a prize to find. If you pass one up simply because you feel the price is outrageous ($350 and upwards), I can only remark that you stand a good chance of never being able to latch onto another. To hope for a market decline on them amounts to little short of whistling *Dixie*.

A couple of years ago, I passed up an opportunity to acquire a fine Colt Army cap-and-ball pistol (1860 model) for one-hundred dollars. Later I finally broke down and bought one—at almost twice the price— to include in my collection. I was tickled to death to secure it, too, at a price somewhat below the market for a specimen in like condition.

What it all boils down to is that Colt Army cap-and-ball pistols, like country cupboards and cabinets just refuse to get more plentiful. The marketplaces simply won't cooperate by suddenly becoming glutted with them. With each passing year, more and more wonderful old Americana gravitates toward private collections, museums, restoration projects, and similar "heritage society" preservation programs, or is otherwise spirited away from prime sources. This fascinating mania we call collecting results ultimately in greater scarcity and, consequently, in higher cash values for Americana collectibles.

13
Old-Time Traps

Every now and then in the course of conversation about antiques, some-one will say to me, "but those things have skyrocketed in price! I can't afford to fiddle around with (this or that) on my limited budget. Tell me: what can a collector latch onto these days that's priced low? I mean, what is there around, not too much touted yet, that will make for a ground-floor opportunity?" If it's a lady, I tell her, "Goofus glass." If it's a gent, I say, "Traps. Find old-time trappers' traps. There's a bodacious opportunity in the offing in this fascinating, but little recognized, byroad of Americana."

First of all, most old traps can still be bought at a low price—perhaps for four or five dollars tops. There are exceptions to this, of course; there are those huge bear traps for example which would be priced higher. However, there are still many rural folks around who'll *give away* old game-traps that have been hanging for years in a shed on the home place, and they're happy to dispose of them too! As for rust or otherwise deteriorated condition on such acquisitions, don't fret too much about that. I'll get to it presently.

Second, there's an almost endless variety to whet the whistle of a buff who's keen on the lore of early trappery. Traps of all materials may be found—not just iron and steel types, but wood, wire, earthenware, and even glass traps! All types of traps add to the variety: wolf, beaver, mink, coon, and gopher traps. If you're lucky you might even locate a

Clay Tontz, trap collector from Covina, California, with an old cage-type rat trap. Smaller models for mice are considerably scarcer.

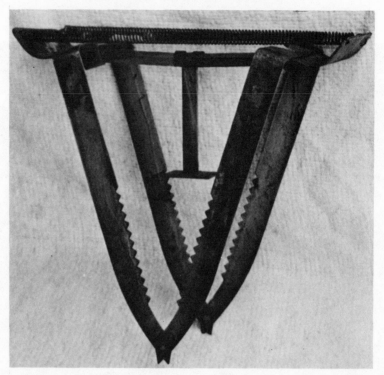

This trap was designed to catch moles. The little animal was supposed to come along and somehow force a clod of dirt upward against the trigger in the center, thereby causing the trap to scissor him.

grizzly trap. In addition to game traps, there are early mouse and fly traps as well.

Third, there's enormous historical significance involved here. The craftsmanship, ingenuity, and overall characteristics that went into the making of many of our pioneer trapping devices puts them in a class with other vintage implements and weaponry that contributed greatly to the development and expansion of the vast frontier.

As to their makers, you'll run into big names along with a sizable smattering of unknowns, simply because there are models of great renown, as well as many weird contraptions that hit the scene with brilliant promise, only to fizzle out miserably when put to the real test. Let's focus on some of the typical ones you're likely to find.

The first few old traps you locate will probably bear maker's indicia such as Newhouse, Victor, or Hawley and Norton. These brands were

Self-Working Rat and Mouse Traps.

Made in two sizes.

A most ingenious invention. Will clear your premises of rats or mice without the use of cats, dogs or poison.

The food boxes, of which there are three, consist of compartments, one on each side and two on top of the passageway (B). These compartments are completely closed, so the bait is never touched by the rats. Therefore, after being once baited they need no more attention, although a small quantity of loose food occasionally strewn at the front door for consumption will prove more alluring. The rat on entering the door (A) into passageway (B) in search of food, sees at the opposite end to the door a mirror which calms his fears as he sees his own reflection, and naturally leads him to believe that other companions are heading for the bait. He passes on toward the mirror, and in doing so passes over a lever which closes the front door and he is a prisoner. He passes on to the passageway (or shaft) leading upward, a wire screen being conveniently placed there to enable him to obtain a footing. He

climbs up the shaft (C) past a trap door (D), which closes so he cannot return. He then passes on to a metal funnel (E), again past another trap door (F), where he finds himself apparently near the outside, as there is a piece of glass inserted at G, letting in light, through which the rat attempts to leap from the funnel. This action causes the funnel to tilt downward toward the tank (H), and reopens the trap door (A), the rat being dumped into the tank (H), which is filled three-fourths full of water. From this there is no escape for his ratship, and after exhaustive efforts he finally succumbs. The door (A) now being open again, the same operation is repeated.

C17194—**Rat Trap.** Weight, 15 lb. Each......................................$4.00

C 17195 **Mouse Trap.** Same general construction as the rat trap shown above. Weight, 2 lb. Each......................$2.00

"From this there is no escape for his ratship . . ." From the ad appearing in Montgomery Ward's mail-order catalog for 1904.

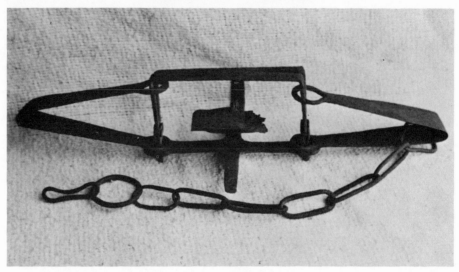

Sewell Newhouse, inventor of the steel trap, pioneered with traps quite similar to the hand-wrought model shown here.

all manufactured by Oneida Community, Ltd., Oneida, New York. That firm produced traps in great quantity for the general hardware and catalog-house trade since the late 1860s. You're not very apt to find any choice rarities in this run of goods—some rather intriguing specimens, yes, but not things one might term terrific.

The trade name Blake and Lamb is bound to show up on items you'll recover. B and L's were (and still are) made by the Hawkins Company at South Britain, Connecticut. This firm, billed as "America's Oldest Trap Mfg. Co.," has been around for more than a century. They were originally set up at Waterbury, Connecticut; so if you should secure an old trap with Waterbury marking on the pan, you've got an item worth much more than one from their South Britain shop.

You'll soon get used to the old-line numbering system employed by manufacturers to designate trap size. No. 0 was about a four-ounce unit, designed to catch wee critters like the California pocket gopher. A wolf trap was usually a No. 4½ size. Newhouse made a trap that would hold a cougar, moose, or the great grizzly bear. It was size No. 6 and weighed forty-two pounds. Skunks, weasels, and the like called for approximately a No. 1½, while beaver enormously strong for their size had to be taken with a No. 4 to assure against breakaway.

In addition to the various sizes there are also classifications as to type:

This wooden pocket-gopher trap, a long-time favorite, has been replaced by a simple, small inexpensive steel model which probably does a better job.

single-spring otter with teeth; double-spring otter; offset jaws; double jaw; "jump" traps; clutch seize; and more.

An old granduncle of mine who lived in northern Ontario trapped successfully for many years using a very elementary spring contrivance called a Stop Thief. He swore by it as the greatest game trap ever invented. Most old timers who ran trap lines had their favorite pelt-getter, I suppose; but Uncle Tony claimed his set of Stop Thief's never failed to fool, and hold, the most trap-wise mink or marten. A badger is a tough customer in any trapper's book, but Uncle Tony took badger with his larger model Stop Thief, too. One time it even caught that legendary bandit of the northland, a *wolverine*; so it goes without saying, no collection of vintage traps would be quite complete without an example of that "sure thing," the Stop Thief.

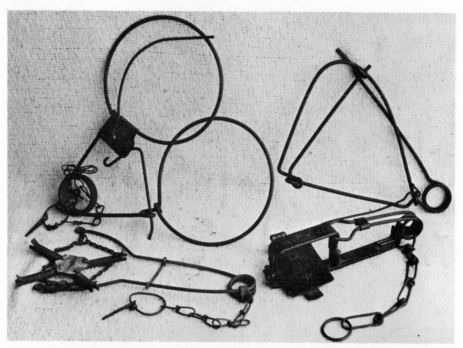

Front, left to right: Verbail trap designed by Vernon Bailey of Washington, D.C.; English small-game trap. Back row, left to right: Oneida Killum trap by Triumph Trap Company; the famed "Stop Thief."

Also, every trap collection ought to have at least one or two nice examples of another worthy trick contrivance, the snare. The age-old Indian deadfall (for which you'd probably have to rig up a miniature replica) would definitely add to the historic value and chronology of a collection of early traps.

Probably the biggest drawback to the collecting of antique traps is that of appropriate display. Because of all the different types and irregular proportions involved, this can be quite a headache; particularly where space (as is the case in most suburban residences) is at a premium. The trap buff who has a basement can work out a rack arrangement of sorts, but by and large a comprehensive showing of vintage traps poses problems.

One collector I know has cleverly solved the problem. He acquired forty or fifty orange crates and stacked them sidewise one atop another along an entire garage wall. Each unit formed a kind of twin-compartment bin to accommodate a couple of traps. His real big traps—a wolf, a No. 5, and a black bear trap, among others—were displayed along the open top of the tiered stacks. Strip molding across the front of each set of bins carried a label showing pertinent data on the traps exhibited therein. He told me that running down that bunch of wooden orange crates was a tougher chore than finding the traps!

The matter of rust on old traps is not as serious as might first be imagined. The exhaustive processing to which producers of quality products put their best crucible steel (special Norway iron was the base) made the metal exceptionally sound and quite impervious to deterioration, except for minor surface flakes caused by prolonged exposure.

Removal of this defect is relatively simple. Pour a can of penetrating oil (any anti-rust solvent) into a shallow bowl. Using an ordinary household paint brush, give the trap a thorough coating, scrubbing oil into the bad places with the heel of your brush. Leave this coating on overnight; then with a stiff GI-type scrubbrush give the trap a vigorous washdown in a bucket of kerosene. Use an old toothbrush to get into the springs and along the jaw teeth, if necessary.

The resulting effect won't restore your trap to mint condition, but it will give it an even-toned, neat and appealing appearance. The well-

Gibbs' long-pan trap pictured above was made for a very special purpose: Mr. Gibbs was plagued with hawks at his muskrat farm in Michigan, and so he designed and manufactured this hawk trap. Since a hawk likes to alight on some high perch to search out his prey, the trap was placed atop the flat peak of a high pole. Thus, Mr. Hawk was caught—hopefully—just as he lowered his landing gear.

worn metal will have what they call patina, a most desirable quality in any antique object.

I'm sometimes reluctant to make bold assertions as to the prospects, investmentwise, in any given area of collector activity. In the case of these early pelt-taking contrivances, however, I'll shout from the rooftops that they're endowed with the strongest potential in the entire realm of pioneer Americana. Let me put it this way: how many fine, old, smithy-forged beaver traps have you seen in important museum displays lately?

The puzzle is *why* these history-laden relics of the mountain man, the bounty hunter, the homesteader, have gone begging, so to speak. To try to fathom this is beside the point, really. One thing's for certain; these old traps just simply refuse to become more plentiful in supply. With each passing year more and more of them go to some kind of happy hunting ground, the place where all good traps go when their days are finally over. It doesn't take real brainwork to recognize that vintage traps, tools of the trade to countless thousands of hardy pioneer settlers, are mighty good property. Value can only go in one direction—and that's up.

If you should decide to hit the trail and go after this particular specie of "game," here's a few tips that might possibly be of some worth as you develop your collection.

Save every old trap you come upon, regardless of condition. The sound components of an otherwise defective trap are of great value in the restoration of a similar model or type. Hold onto all original chains. They're an integral part of the relic and should never be detached or discarded for the sake of convenience in handling or storage.

Build your collection along two lines. A scale-up grouping (No. 0 to 6, including the ½s, of course) and an assemblage of odd-ball contraptions—the ones that follow no specific sizing formula, one-of-a-kinds,

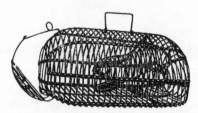

This 1904 catalog clip shows a scarce cage-type mouse trap, a smaller version of model held by trap collector Clay Tontz (illustration reproduced elsewhere in this chapter).

unique things. When you get into this fascinating pursuit in earnest, you'll find traps that no one ever heard of before. These can only be defined in one manner—"humdingers"—and any collection of anything that has a few real humdingers in it, is truly a collection worth seeing and enjoying.

14

Early Sportsmen's Gear

Sportsmen, by and large, are more than appreciators of wilderness trails and remote, rippling streams. They're true collectors, too. Show me a hunter, a woodsman, or fisherman who spends long evening hours puttering with (even caressing) his fine-crafted rifle, some sure-lure decoys, a favorite casting rod—good camp gear of any sort, for that matter—and I'll show you a man who has those stirrings of the soul which bespeak something more than merely that of a possessor of equipment to employ afield.

He's a buff with an appreciation and affection for old-time, well-made things—things with character and quality. He's a collector. His sense of sportsmanship strides side-by-side with his fascination for that peculiar mania we call collecting. Let me cite a few instances where I've come upon the sportsman-collector in his real element—at a campsite—with some essential camp gear he has brought along.

First of all, there's the vintage camp stove. One hunter I know would never think of embarking upon his annual fall deer hunt without packing a remarkable little stove he'd acquired perhaps twenty years previously (and it was a relic then). It's the cutest rascal imaginable, dating from about 1900 called a Happy Rover.

After carefully examining some old merchandising literature, I managed to secure information on that relic from a Montgomery Ward catalog, dated 1904. The little gem originally cost $5.25; a somewhat larger

The Happy Rover.
The best on the Market.

SHOWING DOORS OPEN.

D 9590—The Happy Rover is the gem of all camp stoves—the invention of a miner 20 years in the business; perfection in each detail. Made of sheet-steel, with oven, fire box and legs; the legs can be used or not, as desired. Doors have wrought-iron hasps. The fire-box is lined with corrugated iron, with an interlining of asbestos, which prevents the probability of the fire-box burning out. All utensils can be packed in oven and fire-box. The pipe is made to telescope, and is in 6 short pieces, each 2 foot in length. The entire length of stove is 14 in., 10 in. high, 14½ in. wide; making the fire box 13½ in. long, 10 in. wide, 9 in. high, and size of oven, 10¾ in. wide, 5½ in. high, 13½ in. deep. Weight, complete, 35 lb. Each, at Chicago........................ **$5.25**

D 9595—Happy Rover, same description as D 9590, only larger size. Entire length of stove is 30 in., 10 in. high, 14½ in. wide; oven same size as above; fireplace 16 in. long, 10 in. wide, 9 in. high. Weight, 40 lb. complete. Each, at Chicago........................ **$5.75**

The renowned Happy Rover, a much sought item by collectors of what is generally termed sportsman Americana. Montgomery Ward catalog clip, circa 1904.

model was available for four bits more. Jake wouldn't take fifty times that amount for his; nor would I attempt to dicker with him for it because that old potboiler has become so very valuable to him.

Another vintage item I observed at a campsite near mine in the Boston Mountains of Arkansas was an authentic, old-time chuck-wagon box affixed to the bed of a trailer unit. This one reflected, in every way, the lore of early cattle trails. It was a wonderful thing to behold, doing service as dutifully and as efficiently as it had for years before the turn of the century; and much of its original pannery and reloading tools were still there performing diligent service, as well.

Tinned-iron plates and cups and a most intriguing primitive flapjack flipper were there along with wood-handled knives and forks. The mixing pan for dough, dimpled with a hundred or so minor dents and kinks, was still doing the job with all the effectiveness it was ever designed to do. Also, there were two Dutch ovens; real, trail-christened, cast-iron relics were a 'simmerin' and a 'stewin' one of those savory

This very small Dutch oven (thirteen inches in diameter) is particularly suitable for use by a couple or trio in camp or on the trail. The lid, with hot coals heaped atop, is absolutely essential to the excellent performance of this remarkable item of cookery. Photo from author's collection.

concoctions that were so much a part of the bill of fare at roundup camps on the Cimarron during the late 1870s.

A couple of summers ago, I stumbled into a campsite in southern Nebraska where an old duffer and his middle-aged son had set up camp. He had an array of "stuff" that would make a relic buff envious. An old, and I mean *old* (the earliest model of its kind) bulls-eye lantern—Mr. Dietz himself probably made it—was hung "smack dab" in the middle of his clearing and a coal-oil (kerosene) can nearby had that classic half-spud plugging up the spout. (A half of a potato pressed onto the spout of a kerosene can serves as a spout cap.) Over the fire, some mighty enticing "vittles" were sizzling in one of the oldest cast-iron skillets I'd ever seen. We drank coffee from his graniteware coffee pot, out of blue and white pint graniteware cups. All that fascinating cooking gear added immensely to the enjoyment of our chat. It was a joy and a thrill to utilize those historic wares. Coffee had never tasted better. The "makins" we shared later in the evening made the reverie complete.

These and many other fascinating items of camp gear and equipage show up from time to time throughout those areas where hunters and outdoorsmen venture afield and set up camp. The men (and ladies, too) who maintain campsites and utilize their vintage articles, utensils, and outdoor equipment have come to expect dual compensation from their treasures—and they get it, too. They get, first, effective performance which is always manifestly assured by reason of the remarkable quality

Although the nicely japaned little "Yukon" Camp Stove shown in above catalog clip was sold through Montgomery Ward by the thousands, where are they now? Avid sportsmen are paying fantastic prices to decorate dens and hobby rooms with items such as these—when they're lucky enough to find choice examples. Montgomery Ward catalog clip, circa 1904.

and adaptability of the expertly crafted wares. Secondly they experience that nebulous something every true collector feels—keen appreciation of worth, antiques wise. How rarely one experiences such twofold joy in matters of either business or leisure these days!

All in all these old items of camp equipage, hunter and trapper miscellany, woodsman gear, and the like have captured the imagination of collectors everywhere. A goodly number of these distinctly American collectibles are nudging the exceedingly scarce bracket on advanced lists of items wanted by today's collectors.

Next time you're prowling around a secondhand store, a junk shop, or one of those institutional outlets that employs the handicapped, keep an eye open for vintage outdoorsman items. If you latch on to something worthwhile, you'll have scored on two counts. First, you'll have secured an excellent example of what could appropriately be termed "sportsman Americana." Second, and most important I believe, you'll have a real "podnah" to take along on your next camping trip. The beautiful part of it all is that it will work for you doing its fair share of the camp chores just as when it was brand, spankin' new decades ago.

15

John Rogers, Folk Sculptor

The following is currently appearing in the advertising columns of three nationally-circulated publications on antiques: WANTED. Rogers Groups. Will pay top prices. Write, describing subject, condition. . . .

What are Rogers Groups? Anyone who is familiar with Norman Rockwell's American-genre paintings that were featured for years as cover subjects on the *Saturday Evening Post* need only translate that artist's remarkable social documentaries into plaster. John Rogers was, to an earlier generation of Americans, the social chronicler of the masses; his media was parlor sculpture rather than full-color paintings for a leading weekly magazine.

Art historians are generally agreed that Rogers didn't produce great sculpture, in the sense that his works did not exemplify the highest (aesthetic, perhaps) standards of the craft. All do acknowledge, however, that John Rogers captured, as no one else had, the customs, emotions, habits, follies, the simple drama of everyday incidents in the lives of everyday Americans during the Gilded Age, 1875-1915.

Contrary to the ornate characteristics of the Victorian era with its heavily carved, gilded, scrolly embellishments, where wealth and affluence were manifested in showy and lavish craftsmanship, a Rogers statuary group is apt to be quite sentimental. It will radiate nostalgia. Its theme, of course, will be a simple one. No caption will be required to explain it because Rogers modeled his works to reflect the feelings and interests

119

During the latter half of the nineteenth century it was the rage at social gatherings to discern character by a quasi-scientific analysis of the shape of one's head. Rogers's skill in this 1886 subject entitled Phrenology At The Fancy Ball *makes the practice appear quite believable. Its height is 20 inches; length 9½ inches.*

of unsophisticated, homey people. Is there anything artistically wrong in that?

John Rogers was born in 1829 in Salem, Massachusetts. As a youngster, his bent was toward working with his hands—crafting things. It seems his nimble fingers were particularly adept at fashioning things "in the round." When he undertook the task of making a new weathervane to replace a sorry one atop a neighbor's stable, young Rogers was keen to give his trotting-dog subject dramatic effect from all sighting points, rather than merely settling for a flat, silhouette cut-out of sorts, which was the usual treatment afforded such utilitarian objects. His trotting dog became, in effect, a clever example of sculptured copper. His Bowser had character. Here is a farm dog (like all good farm dogs) that ate well.

Because of a certain naiveté that appears to pervade the manner, or rather, technique of much of Rogers's work, some art biographers have assumed that he was entirely self-taught. This is not entirely so.

Research discloses that upon completion of elementary schooling, Rogers went to work as a dry-goods clerk in Boston. A cloth-house proprietor recognized his sense of design and induced him to make a trip to Spain to select fabrics for exclusive importation. Upon return, Rogers broke away from that profession and began the study of civil engineering with emphasis on the machinist trade. In 1856 we find him in charge of a railroad repair shop at Hannibal, Missouri. The foundry there produced castings for sundry purposes and it was here Mr. Rogers began modeling in clay.

He went to Europe again in 1858, returning the following year to Chicago to enter a surveyor's office as a draftsman. The significant thing about this is that Rogers had, during the stay in Europe, been exposed to sculptors—real, live sculptors—in action. There were dozens of ateliers in operation throughout France and Germany during that time and Rogers wasn't the type to be merely an idle onlooker. Hence, upon return home, we find he made a quick move into the realm of drafting, an essential requirement in the exacting mechanics of producing effective sculpture.

That same year, 1859, he produced his first statuary work to be cast for sale. It was titled *The Slave Auction*, sometimes referred to as *Uncle Tom's Cabin* in plaster. Rogers placed it on exhibit in New York. Contemporary accounts say it was well-received, which was encouraging, but not too profitable financially. However, later that same year he modeled the piece that catapulted him to sudden fame—a wonderful group titled *Checker Players* which he exhibited at the Cosmopolitan Bazaar in Chicago. Hundreds of viewers expressed desire to own a copy of this delightful conversation piece.

The work that brought Rogers almost instant reknown in 1860 was entitled
Checker Players. *The one pictured here,* Checkers Up at the Farm, *is a later version of the same subject and probably his second best seller—over 5,000 copies were sold. This piece of statuary, which then retailed at fifteen dollars, is twenty inches high, seventeen inches wide, and thirteen inches deep.*

A later work (1887) was (the Reverend*) Henry Ward Beecher. This is a typical example of one of Rogers's single-figure statuettes. Its height is 24 inches, length 14½ inches, depth 12 inches.*

The enthusiastic acclaim of admiring crowds at the Bazaar convinced Rogers that he had "clicked." What followed has to be regarded as a foregone conclusion because John Rogers was, in addition to his talent, ability and competency as a craftsman, also a clever merchandiser.

In 1860 Rogers went into the business of producing parlor statuary in a big way. With inspiration and zest he created two more realistic subjects, *The Village Schoolmaster* and *The Fairy's Whisper*. These were heavily slanted toward touching the heartstrings of ordinary folks everywhere. They sold like hotcakes.

Fired with avid dedication now, Rogers embarked upon a career that was to span more than thirty years and to produce eighty different models. He personally supervised his workmen through the several processes involved in the mass production of his groups. Initially, of course, he worked alone, meticulously fashioning, creating his subject in clay. From that model a mold was made which, in turn, was used to produce a bronze casting. The bronze was the master unit from which the final mold of a plasterlike material emerged. This in turn was covered with an oil based paint, usually a tan, putty color or smoky gray; a few were finished off in a somewhat brownish tone, to simulate granite. They were beautiful!

The selling end of it was easy. Display advertising in national magazines did the trick, simply because newspapers of the time heralded each new emission from his studio as a significant event. The groups had price tags ranging from fifteen to twenty-five dollars, depending upon the intricacy (and consequent casting expense) of the particular subject. Each creation was patented.

By 1865, in high gear now, Rogers had twenty-five workmen turning out hundreds of plaster reproductions of each new subject which he personally modeled with his own hands. He "had made it"—a success story in the fullest sense of Yankee ingenuity tradition.

In certain respects the enterprise was a percentage game, for some of his statuary groups failed to capture the public fancy as well as others. On some subjects, a hundred or so reproductions constituted the com-

JOHN ROGERS
NEW YORK

Incised name and place of origin appeared on base of Rogers's parlor-statuary groups. Sketch by author.

plete issue. Needless to say, these limited editions are extremely scarce today. One group, *The Sharpshooters* (a soldier subject done in 1860 foretelling an episode of the impending Civil War) is one of the rarest of Rogers's groups; it commands a small fortune these days. Other themes, notably his series of three Rip Van Winkle anecdotal compositions, sold in the thousands. It is estimated that in the three decades of Rogers's fame, over a million dollars worth of statuary groups were displayed atop marble-topped Victorian tables everywhere in America and Canada. For that era, it was big business beyond a doubt.

John Rogers had done something no other American sculptor had even come close to doing. He had created and developed an appealing line of statuary that people everywhere could understand, could appreciate, could afford to buy—and they did buy, to place in their very own homes. Rogers's accomplishments to this end was indeed a phenomenal one.

By 1892 however, Rogers's star had dimmed. With other gaudy elements of late Victorian decor, his work went out of vogue and he was forgotten. Thousands of his intriguing creations—superb examples of one of our most distinctive Americana art forms—were carelessly stored away, broken, discarded.

Surviving examples of Rogers's groups occasionally come to light from the lofty attics of Victorian mansions of once-flourishing communities throughout the country. No complete collection of his eighty subjects exists today. The New York Historical Society has an outstanding showing of them, nearly complete, numbering seventy-eight works. (In all, Rogers had produced eighty.) Every Rogers buff hopes to stumble on *Camp Life* or *The Card Players*, an 1862 group of which no copy is known; it depicts two soldiers playing cards on an army drum. The other classic rarity is an 1860 piece called *The Farmer's Home*. A fortune awaits the discoverer of either one of these.

The estimated values today of Rogers's groups vary. The pricing guides which list, describe, and assign a fair market value to thousands of items of collector interest appraise Rogers's groups to be in the one-hundred to two-hundred-dollar range. A couple of exceptionally rare subjects may be valued at three-hundred dollars. These prices are (to my way of thinking) just about one hundred percent off target.

Scan over most any antiques publication these days and you'll find knowledgable dealers advertising to the effect they'll buy Rogers Groups at prices quoted in established pricing guides. This means that when a dealer secures a group at the recognized price, tacks on his usual markup, and pays for his advertising (both to acquire more and to sell the ones he has) the going rate now becomes doubled.

Wounded To The Rear *or* "One More Shot" *is an 1864 work, one of several subjects Rogers did during the Civil War years, 1861-65. The standing soldier is removing a cartridge from his case in order to have one more parting shot at the enemy before assisting a wounded youth to the rear. Its height is 23½ inches, length 9½ inches, depth 10 inches.*

Therefore the general rule of thumb on Rogers's prices is: two-hundred dollars or more for a relatively popular subject and up to six-hundred fifty dollars for *Mail Day*, an exceedingly scarce one. All this, of course, is contingent upon that all-important factor governing values of antiques in general—sound condition. It goes without saying, statuary in plaster that has survived a hundred years or more and is still in near perfect condition calls for bonus dollars when the bargaining gets under way.

John Rogers closed his New York studio early in 1893 and retired to his fine residence at New Canaan, Connecticut. He turned his attention to the preparation of anatomical portfolios in the interest of art and busied himself with making garden and lawn statuary for the spacious grounds of his estate.

He was under no disallusionment. He was well-to-do, contented in the afterglow of the achievements he'd scored during his remarkable pro-

This wood engraving, (a very scarce model, as are most Rogers's Civil War subjects) was used by the sculptor in advertising literature to introduce his 1865 subject, Taking the Oath and Drawing Rations. *An intensely moving parlor statuary, it portrays a Southern mother compelled by necessity to take an oath of allegiance in order to receive food from the Federal commissary.*

fessional career, and he was happy in his role as host at social activities with family and friends at home. He died there in 1904.

John Rogers left his mark on America. He had made his statuary "performers" give pleasure to a wide audience and had made a good living at it, too. No artist ought to ask for more.

Bibliography

Beitz, Les. *Treasury of Frontier Relics*. New York: Edwin House Publishers, Crown Distributors, 1966.

Beitz, Les. *Treasury of Frontier Relics*. Revised edition. New Jersey: A.S. Barnes & Company, Inc., forthcoming.

Bristow, Dick. *Illustrated Political Button Book*. Santa Cruz, California: published by the author, 1972.

Drepperd, Carl W. *First Reader for Antiques Collectors*. Reprint. Garden City, New York: Garden City Books, 1951.

Mandeville, Mildred S., ed. *Used Book Price Guide*. Updated and enlarged. Kenmore, Washington Price Guide Publishers, 1966.

McClinton, Katherine Morrison. *American Country Antiques*. New York: Coward-McCann, 1967.

Mirken, Alan, ed. *Sears, Roebuck Catalogue: 1902 Edition*. Crown Publishers, 1970.

Orton, Vrest. *The Famous Rogers Groups*. Weston, Vermont: published by the author, 1960.

Sedlak, Pat. *Antique Trap Collecting*. Belle Vernon, Pennsylvania: published by the author, 1968.

Winchester, Alice. *How To Know American Antiques*. New York: New American Library, Signet Key Books, 1951.

Other References

Montgomery Ward Catalogue: 1904. Reprints available.

Dime Novel Round-up. (Fall River, Massachusetts; edited by Edward T. LeBlanc.)*

*"A monthly magazine devoted to the collecting, preservation and literature of the old-time dime and nickel novels, libraries and popular story papers."

Index